PRAISE FOR *DESIGN YOUR LIFE* and PERNILLE SPIERS-LOPEZ

In *Design Your Life*, Pernille Spiers-Lopez tells the story of an ordinary
girl with an extraordinary life. Her career, including eight years
as president of IKEA North America, was not built on elite-school
credentials, but on common sense. And she makes you feel you can
do that too! The book is rich with Pernille's hard-earned lessons, as
well as ideas on how to tap into your own strength and potential.
She shows you how you can build *your* life
(no Allen wrenches required).

—**Mette Norgaard**, co-author of *TouchPoints*

Pernille's book inspires readers to think about their own unique
dream lives: in relationships, careers, and within themselves. She
takes it a step beyond dreaming, inspiring new ways of thinking
about our current circumstances and potential. She motivates the
reader to create a plan of action that will result in important, realistic
changes. *Design Your Life* offers sound wisdom, concrete tools,
and useful strategies for anyone seeking to discover
and embrace her/his own version of a
good life, designed.

—**Marta S. McClintock-Comeaux**, Ph.D., associate professor, director of
women's studies at California University of Pennsylvania

"Leadership starts with who I am as a person," Pernille writes, as she shares her non-traditional rise in the corporate world. Yet this book is not solely about designing your personal business strategy; it is about the business of "designing the life you want to live." She shares her journey in a very transparent and humble manner, engaging readers in conversation, thought, and tools for following their personal legend. This book is not designed to give a quick fix, but rather, to provide tools to help the reader examine their lives, goals, and paths to travel. I have had the privilege and benefit of countless conversations with Pernille ranging from topics on diversity, social justice, and mentorship, to trying to be the best mothers and wives we can be, all while biking, sitting on a patio, or walking sixty miles to fight breast cancer. Pernille "walks her walk" daily and she shares her personal legend in the following pages with many more still to be written.

—**Nancy Ferguson**, elementary school principal and lucky friend

When I met Pernille I was at a point of frustration. Pernille invited herself into my life at a critical moment, challenged me to look at my life and career in a fundamentally different way, and inspired me to envision and achieve success on my own, out of the comfort zone of a large company. She allowed me to step back from the seemingly disconnected fragments of my life experiences and my career accomplishments and failures, see them as a narrative, and reset that narrative to form a trajectory. In my corporate career, I feel like I've been through it all, every business trend of the moment. But this conversation with Pernille was different—it changed my life in a profound way, and that change continues.

—**Mark Fancher**, founder and president of Parking Advisors

Pernille has been a friend and professional mentor for several years, and her insight and guidance on leadership, accountability, and passion have been invaluable to me and our company. Her story resonates because it is so real—you will not find overnight success or repeated, blind strokes of luck in her story. Rather, hers is a long process of self-discovery with an unyielding foundation of optimism and passion. Her life philosophy of believing in yourself and taking responsibility for your own success is a powerful message for anyone who has felt uninspired or without passion in any part of their lives.

—**Sameer Dohadwala**, co-founder and CEO of Unbranded Designs

Are you in charge of your own life? Do you want to make your dreams come true? Or are you in fact just a blind passenger tagging along on the journey instead of taking control and actively shaping life on your own terms?
These were questions I was asking myself.
Design Your Life is much more than a well-written memoir, it is an excellent and huge source of inspiration for how to play an active part in the shaping of your own life, and making the most of it based on who you are and your core values. It inspired me to live with integrity, to live life on my terms, and for putting my mark on the journey called life, both privately and professionally.

—**Lise Brogaard Falkenberg**, retail director of VERO MODA

I grew up in poverty, believing the only way to survive was through crime, drugs, and violence, and the only way to get out and be successful was through basketball. In my community, it's a tough cycle to break. I just signed a contract and will be playing professional basketball in Europe this fall after four years of college basketball, and I am the first to graduate college on both sides of my family. I am here today, because Pernille taught me the concept of personal leadership and responsibility. Getting here has been a difficult road and I have lived under constant stress and fear of failure and letting myself and my family down. Through mentoring, love and support of Pernille and her family the past five years, I realize I am more than a basketball player, I am a successful man. I feel strong, powerful, and know I will put my degree to use and design the life I want for myself and my family. It is not just me. I am an example—that it can work for anyone. I hope you will read this book and take responsibility for your life. You can achieve your dreams just as I have today.

—**Calvin Newell, Jr.,** professional athlete and "adopted son"

Design
Your
Life

Former IKEA Executive
Shares Her Tools for
Personal Success

Pernille Spiers-Lopez

20827 N.W. Cornell Road, Suite 500
Hillsboro, Oregon 97124-9808
503-531-8700 / 503-531-8773 fax
www.beyondword.com

This publication contains the opinions and ideas of its author. It is intended to provide helpful and informative material on the subjects addressed in the publication. It is sold with the understanding that the author and publisher are not engaged in rendering medical, health, or any other kind of personal professional services in the book. The reader should consult his or her medical, health, or other competent professional before adopting any of the suggestions in this book or drawing inferences from it. The author and publisher specifically disclaim all responsibility for any liability, loss or risk, personal or otherwise, which is incurred as a consequence, directly or indirectly, of the use and application of any of the contents of this book.

The Beyond Words logo is a registered trademark of Beyond Words Publishing, Inc.

The Save the Children logo is a registered trademark of Save the Children Federation, Inc.

The Four Rooms of Change is a registered trademark of A&L Partners AB. For more information, visit www.fourroomsofchange.com. Four Rooms of Change illustration by Lene Simonsson-Berge.

For more information about special discounts for bulk purchases, please contact Beyond Words Special Sales at 503-531-8700 or specialsales@beyondwords.com.

Manufactured in the United States of America

10 9 8 7 6 5 4 3 2 1

Library of Congress Cataloging-in-Publication Data

Spiers-Lopez, Pernille.
　　Design your life : Former IKEA executive shares her tools for personal success / Pernille Spiers-Lopez.
　　　　pages　cm
　　　1. Spiers-Lopez, Pernille.　　2. Businesswomen—Denmark—Biography.
　　3. Women executives—Biography.　4. Career development.　　5. Success in business.
　　6. Self-realization.　I. Title.
　　HC352.5.S65A3　2014
　　650.1—dc23
　　　　　　　　　　　　　　　　　　　　　　　　　　　　　　　2014027949

ISBN 978-1-58270-542-2
ISBN 978-1-58270-543-9 (eBook)

The corporate mission of Beyond Words Publishing, Inc.: *Inspire to Integrity*

For my father, who gave me the gift of confidence,
and was the first person to have complete trust in me
and believed I could do anything.

CONTENTS

Part 4: The Power of Networking and Mentoring

Part 5: My Journey Continues

CAREER TIMELINE

1977:	Graduate, TH Langs Gymnasium, Silkeborg, Denmark
1982:	Graduate, Denmark's School of Journalism, Aarhus, Denmark
1982–1983:	Freelance Journalist, Copenhagen, Denmark
1983–1985:	Founded Royal Danish Import, Fort Lauderdale, Florida
1985–1987:	Director of Stores, the Door Store, Miami, Florida
1987–1990:	Merchandise Manager, Stor, Los Angeles, California
1990–1993:	Sales Manager, IKEA, Los Angeles, California
1993–1997:	Store Manager, IKEA, Pittsburg, Pennsylvania
1997–2001:	HR Manager, IKEA North America
2001–2009:	President, IKEA North America
2009–2011:	Global HR Manager, IKEA
Present:	Board Member, Meijer Corporation, Grand Rapids, Michigan
	Board Member, Coop, Copenhagen, Denmark
	Trustee, Save the Children

FOREWORD

As her good friend and mentor, I knew Pernille long before she was "discovered." Our first meetings were as colleagues, and we were both HR managers at IKEA, Pernille for North America.

I was struck by her lack of the need to be the center of attention. Her small ego allowed for other people to grow and expand their potential. This was confusing for many in the company, especially people who were used to looking to the boss to make decisions. For some, Pernille's way of doing things was a freedom and opportunity to unleash their potential and assume responsibility.

The paradox is that her humble approach often put her in the center.

During her career, Pernille has delivered great business results, improved financial performance and key figures, and under her leadership IKEA USA inceased revenue from $1 billion to $3 billion. Her true joy, though, and her victories in her own eyes have been to see people grow beyond their own imagination.

Over time, I have watched her spending time and effort creating a work environment where people can break through their own self-created ceilings and discover their full capacity. Her insights into what it takes to unleash both her own and others' true potential have grown.

I have now worked with Pernille on both corporate and personal projects for decades, and there are always three dimensions she intuitively brings to the table.

- There is never a ceiling. Everything is possible!
- There is no box other than in our minds. Thinking outside the established pattern will create a better world.

- We should trust in the need and possibility for human beings to expand. We must establish the framework and make sure it does not limit our potential.

I have seen Pernille's life change, but I have not seen a change in these qualities. As her formal power increased, so did the impact of these traits.

I remember a meeting when she was president for IKEA North America and our task was to design a training program for a group of potential leaders. A normal way of doing things would be to produce a complete solution in the traditional framework, with a curriculum, teacher, and timeline.

Nothing of this happened. Instead of producing something, we produced nothing.

A few months later, Pernille entered a stage with dozens of young talented employees expecting her to describe the training program they had been chosen to take part in. Pernille spoke about her expectations of leadership and ended by telling the group that there was no training program. There was nothing but expectations of leadership and a clear understanding of what excellence looked like within IKEA.

The vice presidents who worked under her spoke in more detail about these expectations, and then they all left the room.

I stayed in the room, and during this time, you could have heard a needle fall to the floor as the group tried to grasp what had happened. No program, nobody in charge—but results were still expected.

As the group came to realize that they had to design the training and could recruit the best of the best, the energy slowly returned. After an hour, the room was boiling with energy, and the group members had appointed leaders.

When I met with the vice president of sales afterward, he said, "I have never done so little and achieved so much."

It would have been safer to do a traditional program, but that was not what Pernille wanted. The meeting was a hallmark of Pernille's three qualities:

There was no ceiling. Pernille suggested teachers who were legends in the industry and therefore seemed unapproachable, but everything was possible.

There was no box. The unusual approach gave the participants free hands and minds to try new things.

The participants had already earned Pernille's trust. The group never let her down. They all got a new taste of their potential. The impossible was within reach.

Design Your Life is a powerful and beautiful book. You will learn from it and enjoy it. More importantly, you will know that the impossible is possible because you are imperfect and are acknowledging that not being perfect is the very foundation for achieving your potential.

Yet when you do take charge, you will find that doing so is only a first step. I can already see that Pernille is in contact with a power higher than herself, as there is already a design in place to tap in to, a power bigger than us all.

Carpe diem,
Ulf Caap

INTRODUCTION

I could only see my feet and the red flashing light. I remember thinking: *So this is success? Here I am away from my home, my family, my children, and my life.*

I was lying in the back of an ambulance after having just turned forty, thinking I was going to die from a heart attack—though I had merely collapsed from stress.

This happened in the middle of a very fortunate and successful career. I had just been promoted from store manager to HR manager for IKEA North America and commuted weekly from Pittsburgh to Philadelphia. I had been married to my incredible friend and husband for just a few years. We were raising two wonderful, young kids, and were keeping up with the house, the dog, and lots of friends. But somewhere along the way, I'd forgotten about myself.

Later, I realized this moment was an invaluable gift. I couldn't see it at that moment, and wouldn't for months to come, but it turned out to be a real breakthrough in my life. Success is not about getting higher and higher up the career ladder, running faster and faster, delivering more and more. It is about doing what we love, being good at it, and not losing ourselves in the process.

I don't define personal success by job title, status, money, or possessions anymore, but by being able to stand with both feet deeply grounded in who I am, in my values, experiences, strengths, and beautiful flaws, and embracing any opportunity or challenge that comes my way.

I have a great career and a fortunate life. I left Denmark at the age of twenty-three as a failed journalist with just a work permit, the registration of a Florida company, an entrepreneurial spirit, my

Danish values, and a sense of heading for a new adventure and unlimited possibilities in the United States. Now, I have climbed the corporate ladder, starting by selling furniture for five dollars an hour and moving up to CEO for IKEA North America, global HR manager for 130,000 people, and being part of the IKEA Corporate Executive team for over ten years—many of those years as the only woman and non-Swede. I was with IKEA for over twenty years, and as my responsibilities grew and the jobs got bigger, so did the responsibilities of being a mom and a wife, and the job of just keeping it all together.

I lost myself by striving for perfection as an executive, mother, wife, and friend all at the same time. I have been leaning in, leaning back, standing up, and, sometimes, falling down—all part of the journey and real life.

I wrote this book so I can share these stories with you, what I learned along the way, and the practices I developed to craft a better life by design.

I want to talk about my insights around embracing imperfection, setting boundaries, and prioritizing every day in order to deliver successful outcomes in all aspects of life.

I hope that you will be inspired to take charge of your life, pursue what you love, connect with your values, build on your core strengths, make decisions, and prioritize, so you can unleash your full potential and enjoy an extraordinary everyday life, rather than end up in an ambulance with flashing lights, thinking it is all over before it really started.

So many of us are focused on our careers, and are driving a hundred miles an hour on all cylinders at all times, striving for perfection. It may all have started as a passion and at some point, without our knowing it, turned into an obsession—for some, an addiction. That's what happened to me. I loved what I was doing, kept going faster and faster, taking on more and more. I was unstoppable. I forgot to take breaks, slow down, and spend calm, quality time with myself and the people I love. One day, my body said no and gave me a fake heart attack—an anxiety attack that came from being in denial for a long period.

When I share this story, so many people come forward and tell me that they have experienced something similar. I know there are millions out there who are still in denial and are quietly having similar experiences hitting the wall and hiding how they feel because it wasn't part of the plan.

I meet people every day—whether they are college students, top executives, empty nesters, or people burned out in a job—who are struggling to connect with what they really want to do.

I believe that we all have unlimited potential. Our own minds and the way we think about ourselves are the biggest obstacles we face. I have worked with thousands of people and have seen what a miracle it is when a person discovers their unlimited potential and starts pursuing things they never believed they could.

When it comes to our personal well-being, most of us are lazy. We leave things as they are, even when they are not working. We are often unsure about the unknown, get too comfortable, or think we just don't have the resources and energy to invest in an enjoyable life.

However good we think these explanations are, they are all just bad excuses.

What happens when you are tired of the way your bedroom or your kitchen looks? I know from thirty years in the home furnishings business that we will spend hours making plans for what we want. We find out what we want to change and have a clear objective. We read home magazines, spend weeks deliberating over what color to paint, what kind of furniture, fabrics, and lighting to get; we ask for expertise, invest money, and spend Saturday after Saturday going from store to store or endless nights searching the internet for just the right look that will make our dream come true.

When it comes to personal development and our lives, we don't invest that kind of time and energy. Why not? It is far more important than anything else, so why not act in a way that shows that changing our lives is more important than changing our kitchens?

But if you want real change, you have to invest time, effort, and thought. Find out who you are and what you want. Take responsibility for the work, just as you do when you take on the job of redecorating your bedroom or remodeling your kitchen.

This book doesn't provide seven steps to a successful life or eight laws of effective leadership. It's a toolbox to redecorate your life.

It starts with your very powerful self that has unlimited potential. Amazing things start to happen when you take responsibility for your life. You stop blaming, and feeling small and victimized, and start feeling confident and in charge.

I will introduce you to poetry, a dance, values, and a compass. I will tell you about imperfect mothers and the necessity to confront illusions, and I hope that the personal story of my own downturn will inspire you to face reality and prioritize yourself and your life.

Every chapter introduces you to ideas, practical exercises, and some good advice that I have collected along the way. You get to choose which of the practices you can use to design the life you want to live.

My most important advice: plan your life with your career as an integral part of it, instead of letting life evolve without a clear purpose and intentions. I want to inspire and motivate you, especially if you are tired of waking up each morning on autopilot and going to work and living halfheartedly.

You might be surprised that you have the necessary strength and opportunities to choose the life you want. You can have it, provided you are willing to work hard. I know from experience that it requires substantial effort, time, real commitment, and goals. But it's worth it.

I hope that my experience and my story can give you the courage to find your own way to dance with life. The good news is that you do not need to be fifty-five years old to be comfortable in your own skin—or to have the courage to live the life that you want.

I left IKEA three years ago with no plan B, and I am now following my own advice, using my own practices, and putting together the next part of my life. I have left the Allen wrench and instructions behind.

What are you waiting for?

> "Whoever you are, or whatever it is that you do, when you really want something, it's because that desire originated in the soul of the universe. It's your mission on earth . . . To realize one's destiny is a person's only real obligation. All things are one. And when you want something, all the universe conspires in helping you to achieve it."
>
> —Paulo Coelho, *The Alchemist*

Part 1

POSSIBILITIES, POTENTIAL, AND POWER

There is nothing more inspiring to me than seeing people overcome adversity by finding their power and just believing in the possibility. Not until much later in life have I become more conscious about this and been able to put words to my way of thinking and living. I might just have been born with this view. For as long as I can remember, I have felt a connection to my ability and my courage; I have done what I wanted to do and felt a very strong sense of ownership for what happens in my life. I see the glass half-full, the world full of opportunities, and all of us with unlimited potential, and I have learned to choose to see the positive in even the toughest of situations. I realize not everybody sees life that way and, for some, seeing the glass half-empty is very natural; however, it is possible to shift your perspective, your way of thinking, and discover your own possibilities, potential, and personal power.

1

POSSIBILITIES—THE ART OF SEEING THEM

Tears were slowly rolling down my cheeks. I was twenty-three, and had just boarded the flight from Copenhagen to Florida and said good-bye to my family and friends, heading for a new life and adventure in another part of the world. I was sitting all alone, listening to Randy Crawford's "One Day I'll Fly Away" and gazing out the window, taking one more look at my home country as we were taking off. I was overwhelmed with emotions—both excitement and sadness. Ahead of me was the land of opportunity and a very uncertain future.

The only thing I had was a newly established company in Florida, my work visa, and my Danish design products to sell. I didn't know all the possibilities ahead of me, but I did know they were there and that I had the courage to pursue them.

Certain moments in your life define you. We don't always see them at that time, but looking back, leaving my safe, secure, native Denmark to fly across the Atlantic to a very uncertain future was a bold move and a defining time for me.

I had teamed up with a female Danish friend, and together we created our export/import design business. My friend took the responsibility for our export business that was based in Denmark, and I was charged with the import part and getting the business up and running in the United States.

Before I left, we had spent half a year planning, securing funding, and applying for a work permit. My brother had followed in the footsteps of our great-grandparents and some of their descendants, and had moved to Florida, so that was where it all began.

Friends and family thought it was as an exciting idea and were all supportive, but I am sure they also secretly wondered if it would really work. As a naïve and stubborn twenty-three-year-old, I of course saw a few risks, but ignored them and was completely driven by the excitement of the adventure and the unknown. I focused on the possibilities and didn't worry about everything that could go wrong.

That's the beauty of being young and naïve. It wasn't a straight road to success. There were lots of failures and mistakes along the way, but I created my own version of the American Dream.

MY FIRST GREAT FAILURE

When I left Denmark, I was a newly graduated journalist. In my high school years, I had discovered my love for writing, my interest in people and their stories, and a natural curiosity, which all lead me to apply for journalism school right after graduation. I wasn't 100 percent sure I wanted it or would make it, but I thought, *Why not at least apply?* So I applied, and while waiting to hear, I went on to travel as a tour guide to Spain and London, and enjoyed a great life of fun, partying, and some work.

It was an exciting time for a young woman from the countryside. I had left Denmark with long, curly hair, clogs, and an ankle-length jean skirt. I soon was wearing tight red jeans, high heels, and blue eye shadow, and had pierced ears. I had my appendix removed in a Spanish hospital and fell in love for the first time; meanwhile, I had forgotten all about the pending application. Most people would probably have been thrilled. But for me it was a dark day in my post–high school, simple, fun life when my parents called me home. I had been accepted. I didn't want to go. I hadn't had enough time to figure out what I really wanted to do. I was taken by the carefree life I'd been living, experiencing new things and learning more about myself. For my parents though, this was a nonnegotiable, and they promised I would thank them later. (I did.)

So four years at the school of journalism started. The education system in Denmark is slightly different than in the United States'. *Gymnasium* there is similar to community college here, and most people take a break after graduation from gymnasium, before pursuing a professional school, like journalism, law, business, or medical school. Many of my fellow journalism students (mostly men) already had more work experience and other professional degrees; they were older and better prepared than me and certainly more motivated. Right from the beginning I doubted if this was the right thing for me. It didn't help that when it was time to work eighteen months in real-life jobs, I got rejection after rejection, including a dream job at Columbia University, while my fellow colleagues got exciting jobs as TV, radio, or business reporters. I finally landed a job at a local newspaper, where I got to cover life in a small town of fifteen hundred people. As a dutiful Lutheran girl, I didn't give up and I graduated with decent grades.

After graduation, the job search started all over again and so did the rejections. I didn't land a permanent job and ended up starting as a freelancer. During my short journalism career, I had to part with my illusion of being a journalist who interviewed famous people and wrote feature articles for the Sunday paper. The reality was more covering a bakery opening in the neighborhood, local politics, and little league soccer games.

After a year, I realized that this was not what I wanted, and deep inside, I was still dreaming about exploring life outside Denmark.

As I look back, I realize it was by no mean a wasted time. The education and my short time in the field taught me some very valuable skills that I have used throughout my career and life. I learned to quickly dive into large amounts of information, get an overview, and prioritize without flinching. You get thrown into situations every day that you might not know anything about, but you have to figure them out and gather information. You have to be comfortable not knowing, be curious enough to find out, and have confidence in the process. That is the life of a journalist, of people in leadership roles, and of anybody who dares to do something new and unfamiliar. Journalism taught me the power of curiosity, the ability to see through things, and the skill to make conclusions.

So I never look back and regret my time working in journalism, but like so many others, I made the decision because I was in a hurry to follow the normal timeline. At the time, I was confused and had no idea about my real interests, passion, and values, or what I wanted to do with my life. It was only much later in life that I was forced to clarify these big and important matters for myself.

THE BIG JUMP

It sounds a little too dramatic to say that I saw the light, but leaving journalism gave me tremendous energy—it's that sense of courage and confidence in yourself that arises when you know what you want. Suddenly, it was clear what I had to do.

I was so sure about the idea and excited about the design company that nothing was going to hold me back. So my friend and I worked hard for months to create and develop our idea, make connections with potential design companies, establish our corporations both in Denmark and the United States, solicit and secure funding, and get the necessary visas. I went to Florida to head up the import side of the business.

Although it was a quantum leap to travel to the United States and start our own business, I was confident, determined, and energized. I was comfortable with the idea that it would take time to get settled and build up the business. I was prepared for obstacles and challenges. I was thrilled. It was a whole new set of feelings, much different from the ones I'd had during my struggles as a journalist.

Now I felt the rush of something new. I felt more alive. I had made a decision, and I was on my way.

OPPORTUNITIES = IDEAS

Courage and the ability to see possibilities are, in my opinion, inextricably linked. I am convinced that we each have the ability and power to shift our thinking pattern from half-empty to half-full. During my career, I have worked with many people, who have low self-esteem, don't realize their own capability, or don't have the confidence to take life in their own hands. They are more comfortable sticking to the way things are. In some ways, it is more convenient and comfortable to complain for those people who have chosen to be spectators in their own lives, easier for them to say, "I am not responsible. That is life, and that is okay."

I meet too many people who think of themselves as small and insignificant, too many who are comfortable with the status quo, too many not taking the lead in life, and too few who are daring to take steps into the unknown, willing to explore and experience new things.

I want to inspire you to think a little differently. If you want great things to happen in your life, it requires that you take responsibility and take charge.

Ever since I was a child, I have always seen possibilities in everything. I have always had lots of ideas—not always good ones—and that is still the case. If things go poorly, I think, *What can I learn from this?* If we look at life as a long strip of options and a learning process, we can see new opportunities showing up all the time.

Opportunities create new ideas and possible next steps. You don't have to start with a well-defined, long-term career plan. You can begin by describing for yourself or your boss what you would like from your life or career in the near future. You will be amazed by how much you can actually make happen just by putting your wish into words. Most of us strive to live in the moment, and that becomes easier if you have an idea of and a vision for the future. Consider:

- Where are you going?
- What would you like to do?
- How do you see your future for yourself and your family?
- Where would you like to live?
- What job would you like to have? If you don't know what you want, it is impossible to get support from people around you.

If you describe everything for yourself, it is one step closer to becoming reality. By creating this vision for your future, you preliminarily decide, in your subconscious mind, how your future will be; you set the process in motion and take the first step.

FACE REALITY

For the most part, not only do I see opportunity and find possibilities in everything, but I also tend to see the positive in people before I discover the less good. I also try to turn bad experiences into an opportunity to get something good from the experience.

That is not to say that I skate effortlessly over problems. Dealing with negative situations can be a tough process, which I learned when the initial euphoria of coming to the United States wore off.

Driving around in a car in the United States, feeling free and like the world was ahead of me had always been a big dream. The first two years, I drove sixty thousand miles in my Toyota Corolla, living the dream. I enjoyed and met all sorts of people who were happy to welcome a young, adventurous Dane.

Since I didn't know anybody, I had to cold call numbers out of the phone book to find potential business partners. Despite the great kindness of Americans, I ran into one "no thanks" after another. Since I'm optimistic, I kept convincing myself that tomorrow would be a better day. I started to go to trade shows, getting regular customers and orders, but it still wasn't enough.

Looking back, I could have recognized reality a lot earlier, accepted that the real potential for my business, the setup and the products themselves, was just not there. It took me a couple years before I reached a point where I had to be totally realistic and say, "This doesn't work." At the time, I lost confidence and energy.

Going back to Denmark didn't even enter my mind for two reasons. I loved living in the United States and since I'd moved, my entire family had moved to the States as well.

I was out of money, energy, and confidence. I felt stuck, and the trust I had with my friend and business partner back in Denmark was at risk.

She was in Denmark feeling that I wasn't doing enough, not generating enough sales, and I felt that she didn't understand what I was doing and the struggles I was experiencing. We finally both agreed to close the business and liquidate our few assets. We were both disappointed, disillusioned, and frustrated with each other.

Not only did the company and our dreams collapse, but so did our friendship. It took me many years to get over both. I felt bad that I had spent the money that our family and friends had invested in us. It was a hard-won lesson on the dangers of mixing money with friends and family. It took about twenty years before my friend and I connected again. It was hard on both of us, but today we are back to our old relationship and thankful for the other.

So what went wrong? We were young and inexperienced, and pushed the problems under the carpet just hoping they would disappear. This is when being too optimistic and not grounded in reality is not good. Afterward, I couldn't even tell myself that I should have acted differently, because I had done everything I could. It just was not enough. So I managed to move forward by simply accepting things as they were. It was a huge step and a very powerful approach that I later drew upon extensively and learned to use more consciously.

Some good things also happened during my first two years in the United States. I met a lot of people while I was driving up and down the Florida coast like crazy, and it created new possibilities in my darkest days.

I had, in fact, met a very interesting furniture entrepreneur, who had repeatedly told me to call when I had had enough of my own business and wanted a "real" job.

He was the owner and president of the furniture chain the Door Store. So I called him up and got a job as a salesperson in the flagship store in Miami, Florida.

BRAVE DECISIONS

Even when I was very close to giving up and certainly didn't see a rainforest of possibilities, there was at least the one opportunity at the Door Store, and that's the one I jumped on. If I had given myself time to look closer, I probably would have found many more.

It was not my dream job. But it was a stepping-stone in a new direction.

Today I can see that I did the right thing when I gave up my business and working independently. I simply had neither enough experience and knowledge, nor enough money. And our products just didn't fit the market.

Every time a possibility arises, it is natural for me to say, "Yes, that is a good idea," and I also expect other people to say, "Let's do it," and to be enthusiastic and see the possibilities. Because of this optimism and drive to make it work, accepting reality and moving on was very difficult and a huge lesson for me.

For many people, saying yes is the biggest challenge. For me, it is saying no. It is something I have also paid the price for. Always seeing opportunities and saying yes without facing reality is not good. Being blind to them and always saying no is equally wrong. Life is really about making conscious choices and, at times, challenging ourselves to do the opposite of what comes natural.

When you are faced with an important decision, it is critical that you are clear about what you want and what is good for you. Have the people around you hear you out, test your decision or idea on them if necessary, and notice if you can maintain your enthusiasm if someone reacts with skepticism. Realize that if critics can get you to change your mind, it's probably not a good idea. The opposite is true as well; if you believe in your decision, you will not easily change your mind. After you have clarified your choice, it is important to discuss any changes and goals with your partner and family. Your plans need to fit into the life you are building with the people around you.

"Is this the right decision?" is a question that you have probably already asked yourself many times and will many more times to come. I am convinced that the important thing is not so much the decision itself but more your ability to take responsibility for the situation and take action. If you throw yourself into a new project—be it a business, marriage, or a training—with the attitude that you are your own fortune, you are on track. The important thing is that you take ownership for what happens in your life.

Realizing that you need to take full ownership for your life is the most important step, and can be the most intimidating one, when designing the life you want to live. You become more visible and vulnerable. As soon as you really take responsibility, you can no longer sit in the audience of your own life and be critical of everything that's happening onstage.

I love the many conversations with coworkers, managers, and colleagues about next steps. Most often the conversation starts with "What does the company have in mind for me?" or "What do you think I should do next?" I always respond with a question right back: "It is not about what the company has in mind for you. What do you want, and what are you ready to go after?"

In my personal life, I know I can be annoying to my sisters and girlfriends because I always turn any complaining right back on them with "What are you going to do about it?"

Of course, I do not always take everything in life as a coaching opportunity, but it is surprising how many moments in life illustrate how much easier it can feel to sit back, just expecting something to change and criticizing. I find that many people are afraid of taking responsibility for what happens in their lives, and this can be especially true for women. It is our inability to act and take ownership that contributes to unhappiness, stress, and depression. We have abdicated our own power and given it to the company, the boss, a spouse, a friend, or a parent.

Yes, there are tough times, bad governments, stupid bosses, and spouses who lack understanding, and you can't change that. However, you can change your approach, and if you don't, it's easy to become passive-aggressive and come to see a world where everyone else is to blame.

Your situation can only truly change in the moment you take responsibility, in the moment you are clear about what you want and are able to communicate that to people around you.

Ultimately you have three choices: accept things as they are, change the situation, or leave.

HOW TO TAKE RESPONSIBILITY

But how do you get the courage to stand up and take responsibility? There is no doubt that taking responsibility, being a leader, and going after the life of your dreams comes more naturally to some than others. But you do not necessarily need to be a CEO and stand in front of two thousand people and lay out a vision for a company to take control of your own life. You can, however, assume a more personal leadership role and be part of the solution, rather than sitting back and criticizing. When you take a step away from sitting comfortably in the audience, you go from being a passive viewer to being an active participant.

We all have the tendency to make things bigger and more overwhelming than they need to be. You can start with a small change. It is just like wanting to lose weight or run a marathon—you don't start out running 26.2 miles. It all begins with making the decision. Most of us have at one point or another said, "I can't lose weight." Sure we can; we just don't want to take responsibility for what it means to lose weight.

You build your own world. Can you lose weight? Yes. Can you eat less? Yes. Are you ready to commit yourself to it? That's for you to answer, and when you finally answer yes to that question, it means you are accepting that it is your personal responsibility.

STOP THE BLAME TRIP

Over the past thirty years as a manager and HR professional, I have heard a multitude of excuses for not taking full ownership. Unfortunately, they often come from women. We often feel we are not being heard, respected, or appreciated. These feelings are reality for thousands of women every day, and our biggest challenge is that we frequently don't know what we really want and therefore can't express ourselves clearly.

My experience is that men go through times of denial and abdication as well, but they tend to come to clarity quicker and can therefore better express what they want. Women are more likely to burn inside with frustration or dissatisfaction, which grows and erodes courage.

To accept that some of the truths you have created about yourself are only your truth, not *the* truth, requires the greatest courage. It is very difficult to dare to deconstruct the things you believe.

Take for example the stories we have told ourselves ever since childhood. In my case, one of those stories was that I needed to remain quiet because I grew up in a small town with an eccentric father.

Our parents are very important in our upbringing and have a big part in who we are as adults, but there comes a point when we have to let that go.

There is no question that we are not all raised under equal circumstances, and some are much more fortunate than others, but we can assume responsibility for the life we have today and make decisions for the changes we want or need to make for a better tomorrow.

When we place the blame on our parents or others, we build up walls of excuses to avoid taking responsibility. We have to deal with the past and possibly even mourn losses or pain, forgive, and let go in order to move forward. It's all about accepting ourselves for who we are today and stopping reverting back twenty or thirty years, to the time when our parents were in charge.

If you want to move forward, change things in your life, challenge yourself, and look for a more life-affirming job and more respect—both privately and professionally—then taking personal responsibility and making conscious decisions is required.

TOOL

FIRST STEP: KEEP A JOURNAL

As you start taking full ownership of your life and start designing it the way you want to live it, journaling is the first commitment you need to make to yourself. Your journal will be your best support and a trusted friend. Writing will open your eyes to what's really going on in your life; it will help you reflect and gain valuable insights. It will help you outline a plan for change. I have been journaling for years, and it has guided me, especially when I have had periods of stress, anxiety, confusion, or feeling down. I share everything with myself in the journal and have become more honest over the years.

"Words are a form of action, capable of influencing change."

—Julia Cameron, *The Artist's Way*

1. Find a journal you like. You will have it in your hands every day, so choose it with care.
2. To get things underway, start with writing three pages every day for at least two weeks. (For the first few days, your writing will typically be telling yourself what you did yesterday, but because you have to write three pages every day, you will begin to dig a layer deeper and reflect more consciously. This will happen automatically once you have warmed up and written out the physical and practical happenings in your everyday life.)
3. Write in the morning, when you have just woken up. This is when you are the clearest, before all the day's events begin to arise. Make it a routine.

4. Write freely, without self-censorship. What are you thinking about, and what's going on in your life right now?

5. See the diary as a good and loyal friend with whom you need to be completely honest. After a while, you will begin to see a pattern in what you write. You will notice problems and challenges, and will be able to see where things fit or don't. It will help you loosen up some of the things that are blocking you.

    A friend of mine got scared and uncomfortable when she started to see certain patterns and deeper issues. She stopped writing and shared her fear with me. A few days later, she found a life coach who helped her address her fears. Eventually, she went back to journaling.

    One of my mentees wrote her morning pages for three weeks and discovered that much of her stress was due to a job that wasn't right. She decided to leave, took two months off, and found her current job, which fits her perfectly.

6. Use the diary for all the exercises in this book.

2

POTENTIAL—YOURS IS UNLIMITED

Even if my first business didn't succeed, my new boss at the Door Store saw potential in me. I don't think he thought he was looking at a future CEO when I met him, but certainly he saw a young woman with potential. I know he saw my passion for selling, my passion for the products, my ability to interact with people, and my confidence, maturity, sense of responsibility, ability to act, values, and high work ethic—all qualities that made him interested in hiring me.

When I got my first real job in this country, it gave me exactly the confidence I needed at that moment. The job itself was not that exciting; I was a salesperson in a furniture store and drove an hour each way from Fort Lauderdale to Miami to work for five dollars an hour. It wasn't a dream job. But it was a job and an opportunity.

I did my best at that job every day. I wanted to learn about the business and sell a lot of furniture. I wanted to grow with the company.

After about six months, I felt I was ready for more and called the president, who had hired me, and told him I was ready for a new challenge. I was a little nervous making the call, and his reaction was not what I had expected. To my great surprise, he said, "What would you like to do?"

Looking back, I think he was testing me. The phone call eventually led to me being responsible for a few stores in Phoenix, Arizona, and later for all twenty-four stores in Florida.

We all have unlimited potential and very seldom tap into this incredible resource because we don't see it ourselves, but if someone shows us trust—as my boss did for me—we get a glimpse of some things we may otherwise never have thought we could do.

When I started at the Door Store, I had no idea that I soon would be director of twenty-four stores. I didn't feel prepared, I didn't have the right training, and there were times I wanted to call and apologize to the staff for my terrible management skills. I was totally inexperienced and didn't really know what I was doing. The owner was a true entrepreneur and the company slightly atypical, so it was a great opportunity for me. It was my first chance to develop and test myself as a manager and leader.

Working with the Door Store led to my next opportunity with a new furniture chain, Stor, that had the simple mission of copying IKEA. I had heard about Stor through a furniture representative from one of our suppliers. He thought I had the right profile for the furniture department manager in the new store in California. They flew me out for interviews, put me up in a nice hotel, took me out for dinner, and offered me the job before I returned to Florida.

A few weeks later, I was all packed up, ready for my next adventure, heading by car to a new life in Los Angeles. The excitement felt almost as intense as it had a few years earlier when I had left Denmark.

This was an ambitious start-up company with a lot of very experienced and talented retailers. The job was a challenge. I was constantly trying to keep up and was seldom ahead, but it gave me a very real, solid introduction to US retail, store management, and leadership. It was an important job for me with invaluable learning, but not the best job in my life, and certainly not the best company to work for. Besides the great experience, the absolute highlight was meeting my husband, who worked in the store while going to school to become a teacher.

WHEN THE BOSS IS THE OBSTACLE

Later, Stor was bought by IKEA. When IKEA management finally came to California, the owner of IKEA jokingly said that I was the best asset that came with the purchase. Of course, I was not part of the purchase, but I had applied for the job at IKEA and started as sales manager a year before the acquisition.

I have come to realize all jobs have a honeymoon period. My start at IKEA was exciting, and besides learning the culture of IKEA, I actually felt quite competent and ready for the task. The challenge in the new job was a strange relationship with my boss. Besides being Danish and fitting quite well with the Scandinavian culture, I never got the sense from him that he valued me, trusted me, or saw any real potential in me. I didn't feel good and only later understood that he was a relatively traditional manager and less of a leader. I experienced his general lack of respect for women; at times, he would ask the most awkward questions. I remember once, during a performance evaluation and development talk, he asked me flat out: "Are you pregnant?" I was in my early thirties and had just gotten married, so for him it was a very natural question to ask. He didn't seem to naturally and professionally engage with women, and at one point, he held a team-building session and invited men only. When I began to express interest in becoming a store manager, I could clearly sense that I would never be good enough in his eyes. He did at one time allow me to take an eighteen-month training program because I kept pushing him, but it never felt sincere on his part.

I took it very personal and realized that I needed to find another sponsor. My chance came when there were two vacant store manager positions on the East Coast. I had met and worked with the person heading up that part of IKEA in the United States, and he heard that I was interested in becoming a store manager.

My first IKEA manager was the wrong manager for me, and I was not right for him. I could not see it as clearly then. I was new to IKEA and didn't have much confidence. Furthermore, I had come straight from working at Stor, where the CEO hadn't trusted me either—not so much because I was a woman or because he was unhappy with my performance, but because he was a tough, traditional US retailer, believing that if you don't put in eighty hours a week, you are weak and uncommitted.

Within the span of just a few years, I had met two bosses who could have gotten in the way of my career and life, and they certainly did nothing to support me, value me, or give me any recognition.

So I know how much harder it is to commit to a job when you do not have the trust, support, and confidence of your boss. To give my best, to unleash my potential, and to deliver my best performance, I need to be trusted, valued, and respected. If these essentials are not present, it really cannot work. This is quite possibly the case for most of us. I didn't know then what I know now. I spent many years trying to ignore this, believing it was all up to me and if I would just work harder, it would all be better. It was truly just the wrong fit.

So the great learning from these two experiences was how important it was for me to be a good manager and leader. I give everybody trust up front; I am challenging, very supportive, and very committed as a manager. I will work with others to achieve success, and I will support those people in achieving their goals and dreams. I will also challenge people to see beyond their own limitations.

The retail manager for the East Coast was ready to give me a chance. This was a great example of me being clear about what I wanted and him having trust and confidence in me.

It was the first time I changed jobs at IKEA. The job was a dream for me. Being a store manager is one of the best jobs you can have in the retail industry. You are close to the product, the customers, and the employees, and it's "your" business. Your leadership, competence, and passion for the business are what matters and will be reflected in your performance.

When I have spoken with employees, colleagues, and friends, I have always emphasized the position as store manager as one of the most fun and interesting jobs at IKEA. You have a lot of freedom with your team; you are out in the market, close to the customers; and there is clearly an entrepreneurial energy and spirit. You can manage details, lead a strategy, see people grow, and watch as they discover their potential.

For me personally, the move to Pittsburgh was a big one. First of all, it was a job I had never done before. My kids were two years and five months old, my husband was without a job until he got certified as a teacher in the new state, and we had only been married for three years. I didn't know how to be a store manager, we were both still learning to be parents and to be married, and we had moved far away from our family and friends. It was a great opportunity on all fronts, but it was also very overwhelming. But a great experience for the whole family and for me came out of it all. It was here we learned to be a family, be married; it was where my husband's career took off; and where I got grounded as a retailer and leader. And it was here that I really started to see opportunities, not just in the employees but also in the market and in the company. Pittsburgh was a failing store and there was a very dark spirit there. It was my job to turn it around.

I had to start focusing on the potential and possibilities, looking at challenges as opportunities and turning the negative into something positive that we all could believe in and work toward.

THE VALUE OF SUPPORT

My own feeling of having unlimited potential has definitely been stronger in certain periods of my life than in others. My high school and journalism days were okay, but they were also without a real sense of confidence, energy, or optimism. My first job at IKEA is another example of this kind of work environment.

On the other hand, I clearly remember the feeling when I got the job at the Door Store: it gave me strength and confidence at a time when I had lost most of it. I got a second chance from someone who didn't know me well but who saw my potential. It was absolutely incredible. In many ways, it was a turning point.

The first time I really got in touch with my own potential was when I got the job as HR manager at IKEA North America in 1997, after four years as store manager. I had the same feeling when I later became president of IKEA North America. Both were influential jobs I never even dared to think I would get, and they each gave me a strong feeling that I had almost unlimited potential.

The job of HR manager was again completely new to me. In addition to the traditional work of an HR manager, I was in charge of developing a new HR strategy with a focus on diversity, women, and life balance. It couldn't have been more exciting. These were all topics that I had a great passion for.

The two executives who recruited me into those two positions—both head of HR for North America and president—initially saw more in me than I did in myself. Yes, I have always been driven, wanted new challenges, and worked hard to do a good job, but I have never been focused on climbing the formal ladder or been interested in the title itself. I never specifically looked at the HR position or CEO role as a next step, but they both became natural next steps for me as a leader. Looking back, I had the real breakthroughs and got the big, new promotions at times when I loved my job; had confidence, joy, and pride in my job; and trusted the people I worked with. When you project confidence, passion, enthusiasm, and knowledge while delivering results, it gives the boss all the right reasons to give you a new challenge.

When I became the CEO for IKEA North America, it was not only a breakthrough for me in my career, but also for IKEA—the glass ceiling broke. I was the first woman and non-Swede to lead the North American region, and my background in HR was also a first. It was the perfect moment: my untapped potential met the untapped potential for IKEA in North America.

WOMEN, SPEAK UP!

My story shows how important it is that you meet the right people, at the right time, who understand you and see your potential. But don't kid yourself. It isn't enough to wait for other people to discover your greatness.

In my job as a store manager, I knew there was an enormous need for new initiatives in regard to benefits and compensation for our workers, and I had been very vocal about this to my boss at the time.

A few months before I became HR manager, my boss called to invite me to a women's conference in New York along with other female leaders at IKEA North America. There were only a few female managers at that time. I went with another woman who was an advertising manager. The other conference participants treated us with great admiration for "all the things IKEA does for women."

It was a surprise to us because we did not feel the same enthusiasm and knew we had a long way to go to live up to the image the world had of the company. IKEA was considered to be a workplace with many women leaders and progressive benefits. Compared with traditional US retailers, we were ahead, but there was still a lot to be done.

I was very frustrated and embarrassed to hear people praising us for things we just didn't do. When I came back from the conference, I called my boss, President for North America, and said it was time for the company to start walking the walk. At the same time, there was an opening for an HR manager for North America, which they were having a tough time filling, as they wanted to have a person with business experience. He said that if I was so committed, involved in the topic, and could see the possibilities of creating better conditions, why not assume responsibility for the changes myself? He asked me to apply for the position, and a few weeks later, he offered me the job.

It is important to do a great job, be passionate about what we do, and deliver in the job we have, but it is not enough. We can't sit and wait for someone to discover us or just wait for our turn. We all need to let our organization and our boss know who we are, what we are capable of, and what we are interested in.

Comments like "What do you have in mind as a next step?" or "What does the organization have in mind for me?" are not the best way to take ownership of your career or to show real leadership. It is necessary to be clear and be willing to take on some important projects where you can offer expertise, be visible, and test yourself. It opens more doors if you demonstrate that not only do you see the problems, but you also have real interest and ideas about how to solve them.

When I was CEO for IKEA North America, I had a store manager come to me and ask when he would be in line for the next retail manager/country manager position. He had put in his time, done a decent job, and expressed clear expectations from the company. I was taken aback. He was not a high performer and was not very visible in the organization. We had a long conversation about how he had higher expectations of the company than of himself. I asked him what he truly wanted and what he was willing to work hard for. I explained that I was not impressed with his performance in his current job and didn't sense his excitement about his current position. He had never thought about it that way, and he wasn't actually interested in taking on this new role. He ended up getting new energy for his current position, took responsibility for his performance, and ended up choosing to be a project manager/store manager for a new store in an area he had always wanted to live in.

If you know your passion and desire, it is important that you initiate a dialogue with your boss, colleague, or HR manager, regardless of whether you are an entry-level journalist or a mid-career nurse seeking to have more influence. I have had hundreds of great one-on-one conversations with colleagues, employees, and friends helping clarify what they want and how to get there. I absolutely love facilitating group sessions and programs not only about what to achieve in your job, but more importantly, what you want in your life.

It is so inspiring to watch when someone discovers their potential, decides what to go after, and then makes it happen on their journey through life. The best emails or letters have been when people tell me afterward that they have decided to become leaders of their own life. This is, in my opinion, an important first step. You will find your motivation and inspiration when you have clarity and are able to state it openly. Then you will start taking action in your daily life. Leadership doesn't happen in a conference room. You have to take a job with responsibility in a specific area and for leading others. You have to translate your passion into something practical. Otherwise, your enthusiasm can evaporate soon after participating in any program. These types of conversations I have had with my bosses helped my development and allowed me to set new objectives and proceed with enormous enthusiasm.

When I moved to the United States as a twenty-three-year-old, I couldn't have imagined the life I have now. As I sat in the plane, crossing the Atlantic, my dreams revolved mostly around feeling free and exploring a new world, starting new and leaving my baggage behind.

I have gone through life being more inspired by my experiences and dreams than I have been concerned about achieving a specific position. As a starting point, I dared to take personal responsibility, and when, along the journey, I connected with people who saw my potential, the path was paved for the life I have lived. It all really begins when we have the courage to follow our passions and dare to unleash our true selves.

TOOL

DARE TO MAKE A CHANGE

"Our doubts are traitors and make us lose the good we oft might win, by fearing to attempt."

—William Shakespeare

1. Making a decision to change something in your life is empowering and energizing. It is not important if it is a small step or a big leap; it is the decision to act that matters. Fear is the enemy of change.
2. Dare to take a step into something new. It's a bit like taking a mental stretch. You extend yourself and leave the familiar, your comfort zone.
3. Accept that any change has its challenges. There will be great learning along the way, and the outcome will be worth it.
4. Spend some time considering what in your life you want to change. If there is a part of your life you are not happy with, doing nothing about it is actually the bigger risk. Consider in what area—health, relationship, work, social activities—you want to make a change. Describe for yourself the end goal, the desired outcome of the change you want.
5. Decide on and make a realistic plan. You might want to start with a relatively small change that you feel confident you can make happen. If you haven't been a runner, you don't start with a marathon; start with a 5K.
6. Write it down. Identifying milestones is important and can make the journey easier. Set specific daily, weekly, and monthly goals.

Share your decision and plan with a close friend or family member to test your commitment and get a reality check.

7. Follow up regularly and make necessary adjustments along the way.

8. Anticipate that there will come a period when you will become disillusioned and frustrated, and will be ready to give up. It doesn't matter whether you started a running regimen, got a new job, or are taking courses in Spanish. After the honeymoon is over, keep at it every day; keep the end game in mind. Remind yourself that any worthwhile change is hard work. You have to stay committed and focused, and visualize how it will feel once you reach your goal.

9. Once you reach your goal, celebrate.

3

POWER—HOW I FOUND MINE

"Our deepest fear is not that we are inadequate. Our deepest fear is that we are powerful beyond measure. It is our light, not our darkness that most frightens us. We ask ourselves, who am I to be brilliant, gorgeous, talented, fabulous? Actually, who are you not to be?"

—Marianne Williamson, *Return to Love*

I was thirteen and in seventh grade. Who knew that a moment in such an awkward stage of life would be so defining and significant? I remember everything about it and especially the feeling of being important, strong, and powerful beyond measure. The curtain was about to go up for the premiere of our school play with a packed theater of eight hundred people. I was on the other side, ready for the opening monologue as the leading character in the classical Danish play *Jeppe on the Mountain*. Everybody was nervous, all panicking—even the director, my dad—all wondering if we could pull this off, and all looking to me to perform the opening act with success.

As I stood there alone onstage, ready for my first real performance, I remember my father asking me, with a bit of doubt in his voice, if I was ready. I was nervous, but as I imagined the full audience on the other side of the curtain, looked at my father and all my classmates, I knew I could find the strength somewhere inside me. For a second, I connected with my inner strength and voice that was telling me I could do this and more. I looked at my father with a smile, and with confidence answered, "Yes, I am ready. It's show time!"

Normally, the annual seventh-grade school play was nothing big, performed only once at the school gym. My dad, who loved theater, acting, and directing, wanted to participate now that his daughter would be in seventh grade, so he volunteered as the producer and director, and he wanted it to be an important, classic play, and he wanted to take it to the nearby city theater. He even organized a class trip to the capital of Denmark, Copenhagen, so we could see the play performed by an incredible cast. I even got to meet "Jeppe" and get some invaluable advice from the master himself.

This was a great opportunity for my dad. He was a very creative man and had a great passion for theater. As a kid, he worked in a big Danish theater and admired the many great actors he met along the way. He was especially proud of a personal note he had from Laurel and Hardy. He had a few minor roles during these childhood years, but he never pursued his dream, his true passion. Though he wasn't afraid to take chances, was always full of good ideas, and didn't worry about what others thought of him, he compromised his own dream and chose a traditional and secure career as an ophthalmologist, mostly to please his parents.

My life leading up to the school play had not been fun. I often felt different, nervous, small, and inhibited because my father and my family stuck out from the norm in this very small, rural community. I got many comments because we lived in a big house, had fancy cars, and often traveled abroad, including going to visit my father's family in the United States. This was at a time when a trip to Copenhagen was still a bit of a big deal.

My father also wrote letters to the editor in the newspaper, and if that wasn't enough, he joined a very controversial political party.

I grew up always feeling afraid that someone would say something about my father, always worried that he would do something embarrassing and sensational—and he often did. As a middle schooler, I thought it would be perfect to have parents who didn't attract any attention.

My father's and my time working together during the preparation for the school play became a real turning point in our relationship. Somehow, I realized that I could not change him, and I discovered some great things about him, and started to embrace and appreciate him for who he was. Perhaps that was also the beginning of accepting myself for who I am.

So the moment before the curtain went up was significant in many ways. Later in life, I have looked back at this moment when I first thought of myself as a leader, discovered my true strength and personal power. I had courage I wasn't even aware of, and I was able to push beyond what I had ever imagined. I dared to be myself and gave it everything I had.

When we talk about power, we often talk about formal power or the power other people have informally over us. What has been life changing for me and truly empowering is discovering my own personal power, my core, my true strength that is unique to me, something no one can take.

I have relied on this Jeppe moment many times throughout my life. I have been standing in front of thousands of people during my career at store openings, as a keynote speaker at conventions, or receiving an important award, and felt nervous and in doubt. I have had moments of complete discouragement and insecurity when our business was down double digits several months in a row, when we had to make drastic changes in the head office, when I had to show up to a deposition in a lawsuit of a wrongful termination, or when I ran my first 5K and wanted to give up with just 1 kilometer to go.

We all have Jeppe moments, and once we know them for what they are and know how to tap into them, they are our lifelines and help us build the life we want.

Both at work and in my personal life, I have watched people discovering their moment of power. A colleague from the Pittsburgh store always wanted to be a store manager, but there was always something holding her back—her family situation, lack of performance, and lack of confidence. Her desire was there, though, and she never gave up. We never lost touch after I left the store, and one day, she became the store manager of a new store in New Haven, Connecticut. I will never forget her opening remarks, her confidence, her pride and reconnection to her long-lost personal power—her New Haven Moment.

When my son was sixteen, he asked my husband if he would run a marathon with him. It was a huge commitment for both of them, and they trained for months together. As we got up at five in the morning on the big day, they were both so nervous. We didn't talk about the rain outside or the humidity that had activated both their allergies. They had a good start, and I followed them in pouring rain to mile ten. Hours later, I was anxiously waiting at the finish when I saw my son coming in—but alone. My husband was not there. At mile thirteen, he had started getting cramps and told my son to run ahead. My son hesitated, had an emotional moment, and finally went ahead. After a mile, he was exhausted and discouraged, and he fell down, throwing up from dehydration. But he managed to pull himself up thanks to Gatorade and a strong belief that he could do it. In the end, he finished with confidence and power. This is a moment my son goes back to when he is down, confused, and full of self-doubt. This is his Marathon Moment.

For my sister, it is the 40-Percent Moment. She was diagnosed with an ugly cancer a few years back and was told only 40 percent of the patients with this form of cancer live beyond five years. She was shocked, stunned, scared, and mostly frightened by the thought she would not see her kids graduate from high school. After a few days of suffering, mourning, and reflecting, she decided to be part of the 40 percent—and she is.

I call this our personal power. There are many words and concepts for this, but the key is to know it exists in you.

Throughout my career, I have been given formal power many times in terms of formal job titles, and have had to accept both the authority and responsibility that comes with that. There are many ways to exercise this formal power. For most of my leadership career, I have made it a point to use the formal power as little as possible and let people around me discover their own power and take personal responsibility.

It is so important to find your power and keep connected to it because it's you, your core. And there is always more of it where it comes from. It gives us necessary confidence and strength that we can build on and tap into when necessary. Our personal power prepares us to face anything in life without losing ourselves.

We each have it. Maybe you have abandoned yours, forgotten it, or not yet found it. If so, you need to start looking for this and connecting with your Jeppe moment.

WHAT DO YOU REALLY WANT?

To decide what to do with one's life can be such an overwhelming question. I didn't have any sense in high school or immediately after graduation about my general interest or direction. My first job, as a tour guide, was a great chance to get away from home and get the party craze out of my system.

My interest in leadership and influence showed up much later, only after I had become a journalist and decided that journalism was not right for me.

Our power becomes more obvious when we know who we are and what we want, and we stand by it.

Personal power is about finding the courage to live the life we want. It requires us to have a general direction for what we want to do. You get strength and confidence that open up unlimited possibilities, and things seem to fall into place a little bit easier.

I know friends, family, and colleagues who persist in living a life that isn't really what they want, but is safer than making a change. They don't dare to imagine what will happen if they take another path. If you are uncertain or unclear about what you really want, you are probably very confused about why things never really work out for you. But how can you expect great things to happen in your life if you do not even know what you want?

I know it well myself. I could easily have gone on to work as a journalist, applying myself to become better and better in that job. I would most likely have made a good career and had a good life, but I would always have had a voice inside me asking if I was really doing what I truly wanted.

It is much easier to continue on the same path. If you make the jump, there is no way to know the outcome, and you have to listen to the inner voice that wants to be heard—you have to trust your feelings are real and worth following even if it looks hard. Just wait. The courage to follow your desire will give you energy and a sense of being in control. As Paulo Coelho says in *The Alchemist*, once you know your personal legend, the whole universe conspires to help you achieve it.

If you are unsure of what direction you want your life to take and what you want in it, know you are not the only one and there are many ways to figure it out. Usually you will be able to find the answers in yourself, often by looking back and connecting to a specific situation. Think of when you felt confident and on top of the world, powerful and strong—when you felt in charge and didn't care what others would think or say. Or think back to a time when you were down in the dumps but knew that you could not move forward if you didn't take responsibility. Those are the moments when you tap into your strength, your power; those are the moments when you step up and manage to change a difficult situation. Those are powerful experiences that will guide you and help you decide what changes you need to make.

DARING TO TAKE A STEP

I understand why many people are afraid and don't dare to take a new step. We all have a fear of failing.

A highly effective exercise is to ask yourself: What is the real risk of taking a major new step? What happens if it does not work out? What are the consequences of doing nothing? The risk of doing nothing can sometimes be bigger than doing something you really want.

If you choose the safe, easy road, the result will usually be quite predictable, and while secure solutions may feel comfortable, they will most likely not change your life. My experience tells me that the risk of moving forward is often less than the risk you take by not doing anything. You can be sick, stressed, burned out, and powerless in your own life.

Real, lasting change doesn't come without hard work. There is no way around it. What are you waiting for? Only you can define what you want, what you dare to do, and what you are willing to invest in.

Of course, there are times in your life where you have to stay where you are. Sick parents or a new baby or myriad other things are certainly valid reasons for staying in a situation, but generally, we are all ready to make a lot of excuses for ourselves for not getting started. You can always find a good argument for not changing jobs, just like the weather isn't always going to be "good enough" to head out for a run.

If you don't take chances in your life and grasp the possibilities along the way, how in the world can you expect things to get better?

The safe, risk-averse approach to life can be compared to going on vacation to the same place each year. The weather may be a little different, you may meet some new people, but basically it is the same from one year to the next. Maybe that is perfectly okay for you and not at all wrong, but if you suddenly travel to India rather than to Greece, you will see a whole new world.

That is also how it is with your personal power. It is your own journey toward more inner strength and power over your situation. Every time you take a step into something you have never done or haven't ever dared to do, you discover something totally new about yourself.

Like me, you will probably find it incredible when the feeling of insecurity and stress disappear as you dare to venture out a little more than usual. It will no longer feel overwhelming, even if you don't have all the solutions. When I landed in the United States, there were still many unknowns in my life, yet I had the feeling of being in control. No one was giving me orders. I had the responsibility and was not dependent on others. I had the feeling of power. And so I was prepared for all the hard work and challenges that lay ahead. It was all worth it.

TOOL

FIND YOUR POWER

This is a practical exercise to find your personal inner strength (your Jeppe moment), which you can tap into both as a lifeline and to help you build the life you want. When you take personal responsibility for what happens to you and your life, you feel more freedom and power.

1. Think back on a concrete situation when you felt confident, on top of the world, and ready for any challenge. You could feel it in your gut, almost like a rush. You were in charge and what others said or thought didn't matter. You stood tall and confident. Describe that situation in your journal.
2. Think back to a time when you were completely down, like in a deep black hole, and got yourself out. Think back to connect with how you realized that it was only you and your inner strength that could bring you back up. You were the only one who could decide what to do. You tapped into your strength and your power. You stepped up and managed to change a difficult situation. Describe the situation in your journal.
3. What can one or both of these situations teach you about yourself? Can you use concrete words to describe your emotions, your strength?
4. Check in now to see how you feel today—with your job, with your family, with your partner, with your health. In what areas of your life do you feel that you have control? How and when do you feel strong? Reflect on how you can transfer the strong feelings to areas of your life where you do not feel as strong, powerful, and

at ease. Hold on to that strong feeling and fill yourself up with it. If you are aware of the areas of your life where you feel at ease and happy, it is much easier to transfer this to other parts of your life where you do not feel quite as strong and happy, and are not living with a clear intent.

If you feel good in some areas and not so good in others, or if you are having a tough time connecting and finding your power moments, don't give up, be patient with yourself, and keep trying. It's there.

Part 2

YOUR OWN JOURNEY

*"No matter how many detours and adjustments it made,
the caravan moved toward the same compass point.
Once obstacles were overcome, it returned to its course,
sighting on a star that indicated the location of the oasis."*

—Paulo Coelho, *The Alchemist*

4

DROP THE LIST OF SHOULDS AND
EXPLORE YOUR OWN PATH

"**I** had a dream to be here one day, so here I am at Columbia University. But the journey to get here has been slightly different than I expected." This was my introduction to seventy MBA students at the very university I had dreamed about as an aspiring journalism student.

Back then, I had applied for an internship but had been rejected. Now I was president of IKEA in North America, and had been invited a few times to come and talk about the IKEA concept and business model. The students thought it was a pretty funny story, and they liked that I did not take myself too seriously and that I revealed I had been rejected but had made it there as a guest speaker.

The same thing happened to me at the Danish financial newspaper *Børsen*, where as a journalism student, I had been rejected first for an internship and then later, as a newly graduated journalist, for a permanent job. Their Executive Club invited me as a guest speaker in 2009, just after I had become IKEA's global HR manager.

Both examples highlight for me that we sometimes reach our goals in ways other than we had imagined. My career has been characterized by not having your typical career plan. There was a path I was expected to follow as a journalist, like for any other job, but when that didn't work out so well for me, I dropped the "should" list and started my own journey.

If you have an overly detailed plan for the next ten to fifteen years, you probably won't discover the options and see the possibilities that appear on the road. Maybe you will reach your highest goal and think, *What now?* Or if your plan does not happen, you might get sucked into a downward spiral.

In fact, I am grateful to the people at the newspaper and Columbia University who told me no. If it hadn't been for those rejections, I would not have had this fortunate life and exciting career.

At the time, those rejections and a few others hurt and affected my self-confidence. I was disappointed, discouraged, and lost. I wondered if I was ever going to make it both in journalism and in life. They were humbling experiences, which most of us go through and get past. They forced me to rethink what I really wanted, and it wasn't to continue with more education, which was certainly a recommended option back then. I didn't have the drive to be educated for education's sake. I was—and am—more of an experiential learner, learning by doing, and have been driven by my passion for adventure and possibilities.

On paper, I haven't necessarily had the "proper" training or background for the jobs I have taken on, which is something that journalists have often taken interest in: the store manager who became North American HR manager without HR experience, the CEO without an MBA or financial degree. I have never let that hold me back. I feel the very essence of this country is that we all have the freedom and responsibility to do what we want; we pursue our own happiness. There is room for entrepreneurs and brave people to take chances and run with ideas in a field they are not necessarily trained in. So why create unnecessary limitations for ourselves?

With my specific background, it was especially interesting to talk with the MBA students at Columbia University. I don't have a degree from this great university, but that day seventy students were fascinated and engaged in hearing about IKEA, how I had reached my position, and what I had learned along the way.

THE MEANING OF REJECTION

Maybe it is a little difficult for others to see or understand from the outside looking in, but from my perspective, there is a red thread of destiny running through my life that is my approach to rejection and failure. When things didn't work out the way I had expected, I was able to adjust, see new opportunities, and take an alternate route if necessary. I have never been afraid of trying something new, and it has benefitted me. When you think back and reflect on your life's rejections and failures, what is your red thread?

Adventure has been my motivation from my earliest years. I have always liked to write about what I saw and experienced. When I started journalism school, it was my dream to travel and write features for a big newspaper.

I am an entrepreneur by nature. I like to start things, and my head is always spinning with new ideas. When I decided not to slog it out as a journalist, my entrepreneurial drive propelled me into the business world. My interest in design and love for leadership and people has also always been a natural source of energy.

I believe that no matter what happens to us, it's a valuable experience; it's an opportunity, and we can choose to get something positive out of it. For those who get discouraged, I say: take a few moments to mourn, then dry your eyes, focus on the learning, and look forward.

To find something positive in a frustrating situation requires a conscious mind-set and action. It's easy to get sucked into a downward spiral. It may seem obvious and convenient to say, "Aw, now that I didn't get what I dreamed of, nothing matters." Instead, see that adversity as a challenge. For me, the rejections made it clear that it was not the way I wanted to go. This does not mean that all refusals need to prompt you to switch your direction altogether, but they will at least allow you to reflect, adjust, and look for other opportunities. I believe anything worthwhile takes hard work. The successful marriages that last a lifetime, the job you love and are good at, and the close friends you have had since kindergarten didn't come without some disillusions, struggles, and problems along the way.

Some people are fortunate and are naturally wired to spot the good in every situation, and so they catch on quickly to new opportunities and move forward easily.

I believe the opposite to be true as well. Some people see the negative in everything, but they can learn to think more positively. It requires a deliberate reprogramming of our thought patterns. Practice releasing the negative thoughts. Take a step back and apply your energy to what moves you forward. As my friend and mentor describes it, "Every thought we have is a conscious choice, and it is either shrinking or expanding." As I have mentored colleagues, friends, and coworkers throughout my life, I have found this to be so true, and people feeling down, with little self-esteem, courage, and energy, share with me that most of their thoughts during the day are shrinking, not expanding.

The ultimate danger of negative, shrinking thoughts is that they can lead to an unhealthy, self-created reality, which serves no good, especially not ourselves.

Refuse the thought that you are "no good/a failure" when you are met with rejection and adversity. Consider instead what you can learn from the specific situation and what you will consider next time; then, focus on your strengths and think about what is next.

Receiving a rejection has always required me to work on myself, and I have had a few pity parties, but they were short, and I did not spend a lot of energy thinking about whether I had the wrong training or was not good enough for the job. Instead, it has presented me with an opportunity to learn what I could do better next time and to remind myself that I have the ability to do anything I really want—this just wasn't the right thing.

THINK BIG AND FORGET THE DETAILS

Our drive for perfection plays a big role here as well. We can't do everything to 100 percent perfection all the time. Perfection is an illusion. My mother has always called me a *sjuske*, a Danish word for not being perfect, cutting a few corners. The requirement of 100 percent perfection leads us down the same dead end as the negative thoughts. Relax the perfectionist demands you place on yourself, embrace imperfection, and feel a huge relief.

When it comes to my job and the important aspects of that, I am detailed, and I follow up, meet deadlines, and set high expectations for myself and others. I'm the same at home. I pay bills on time, keep a very organized house, and follow recipes down to the smallest details when I am cooking new dishes—but I am not a perfectionist drowning myself in details. I always come prepared to meetings, but if you have two hundred pages of documents to go through, it is important to prioritize and be prepared for the critical agenda points and accept the rest just won't get the same attention.

By prioritizing and letting some details go, I can save a lot of energy: I can pack for a trip in an hour, and if we have guests for dinner, I can say, "How long will it take to cook this? How long will it take to do the shopping? Okay, so I don't have to even think about it before three o'clock." For me, there is no need to be planning days in advance. I realize that doesn't work for everyone.

One time, my family and I were driving to South Carolina on vacation. I was the assigned navigator. The day before we left, I looked at the map and realized it was a simple route: we needed to go south on I-95 and then east on I-26. I figured we would stop for lunch, dinner, and hotels as we saw fit along the way. Heading out the driveway, my husband asked, "So, what's the plan?"

I showed him the map and said, "We need to go south for two days on I-95 till we hit I-26, then go east for an hour."

That surprised him. For him, navigation had more details to it, like how many miles a day, booking hotels along the way, and breaking the route up into smaller pieces. Despite our different approaches though, we still made it to Charleston, South Carolina.

Make plans and be super-detailed when it is necessary. It is really much easier than you think. Even though on paper I wasn't "qualified" to be the head of HR in North America or CEO for the entire organization, making plans, prioritizing, and letting some details go were part of how I was able to do so. It was a matter of believing that I could jump into most anything and figure it out. That is one of the good things I got from my childhood and from my training as a journalist: I learned to focus on the big picture and forget the unimportant details.

Unfortunately, I see many women, including myself sometimes, who focus on the things we can't do, the missing qualifications for the next job, or the work we didn't do to perfection. It has often surprised me that we want to get ten out of ten correct just to think we have passed a test. Many men pat themselves on the back when they get eight right because does anybody really need to focus on the two things that were wrong? If it is okay, it's most likely good enough. But women can easily focus on the two that were wrong and lose track of the fact that we have actually done a major part of the task. If everything has to be 100 percent perfect and every little detail needs to be in order, we stress ourselves unnecessarily and will never feel that we are doing anything good enough, will never take on great new challenges that we are more than qualified for.

If we exclude very specialized subjects, we can transfer this kind of mind-set to most jobs, especially leadership positions and larger companies. It is usually not crucial to have a lot of the specific knowledge, but it is necessary to have the ability to navigate, think critically, and lead the organization. We don't need to know everything, but we do need knowledgeable people around us, and we need to gather the relevant data and information, set the direction, ask the targeted questions that a situation requires, and make decisions.

In the same vein, you want to release the urge to plan each and every step of your career path in advance. Of course there are some steps that, realistically, can't be skipped. I could not have been CEO of all the IKEA stores in the United States if I had not been a store manager. On the other hand, I didn't first need to be HR manager to lead IKEA North America, although it gave me great experience and helped me become visible to the CEO, who chose me as president of IKEA North America.

Mine has been a career that evolved organically, and it's taught me that an overly detailed plan can actually do more harm than good in life. First of all, it can blind us from seeing new opportunities along the way, and second, if we are too goal oriented, it is easy to separate work from the rest of our lives. I believe it is healthier and more sustainable to make work an important, integral part of our lives, but not our life in and of itself.

DON'T BE A SLAVE TO YOUR CAREER

A friend asked me to dinner because she needed help. She had almost become a slave to the action plan she had for her career. It turned out that she needed to get rid of a lot of assumptions and unrealistic expectations she had created in her head. She had created a career plan and couldn't imagine deviating from it even in the slightest. She was asking me for permission to break it and to think differently. While the ambitious career plan she had created was perfectly fine, the issue was about timing; she was trying to achieve her lifelong goals in just a few years. In her rush to reach her career goal, she had forgotten to develop other sides of herself and her life, and that turned out to be the real cause of her stress. She knew the answer but needed someone else's permission to slow down, evaluate, prioritize, and move forward at a more realistic pace.

Early on, we might have a feeling of urgency or pressure, and getting a good education is important. But not all Nobel Prize winners attended Yale, Harvard, or Princeton, and most of the rest of us who didn't ended up with excellent lives anyway. Remember that there are multiple paths to success. What else would you like to do? Do you dream about a different job or a new challenge?

A young interior decorator I worked with in Pittsburgh is a good example of this. She was an excellent interior designer when I was store manager. She sought me out when she saw that the job as the head of her department was available. She knew that a management job can be a quick way to success, but she was uncertain about going for it. Her ambition was to have a successful career, and she wanted to know if I thought she should apply for the job.

In response, I asked her about her passion and where she saw herself in five years. She was unsure and confused. I asked her to think about it and assured her that confusion was okay. The next day she came back expressing a sense of relief because she was fully aware that her passion was design and not management. Instead of focusing on the open management position, we talked about plenty of other opportunities for development in her specific area of interest: interior design. A few months later, she moved from Pittsburgh to Philadelphia, where she became the lead interior designer for the North American expansion team with responsibility for planning showrooms in all our new stores. She later became the manager for the entire visual merchandising and interior design team in one of the new stores in California.

She said no to what was the "safe career path," and instead followed her passion and became successful on the route that suited her. She took the same management position some years later, but did it her own way and at her own pace. It involved, in her case, a gentle push and daring to say no to the usual way forward.

Daring to say no is often a strong way to choose your own path. The reverse can also be true. I have met others who came close to saying no because they did not see their own strengths, didn't believe they could handle or cope with a new big step, even though they really wanted it. Sometimes we look a little too narrowly on our potential, because we are locked into a self-image that typically has little to do with reality.

I believe it's a lot about timing. When we opened our store in New Haven, Connecticut, I was very proud that one of my mentees was the new store manager. I knew it had always been her dream. We had worked together when I was in Pittsburgh and we were both struggling to find balance in life. She always put family first, and said no to promotions, so she could be there for her daughter, parents, and husband in his career. She worked in Pittsburgh for fifteen years, helped to develop a lot of IKEA managers, and was always motivated and willing to learn and develop herself. For many years she knew that she would like to be a store manager when her daughter went off to college. It was a great moment seeing her dream come true.

She had always kept the possibilities open—for her it was just a matter of timing and saying no until she knew it was the right time.

ZIGZAGGING FROM A TO B

My personal experiences, in life in general and as a leader, have convinced me that there are many ways to arrive at the same destination. I was often in charge of executing a business plan that would get us from point A to point B, but it was never as simple as following a straight line. I knew that, most likely, we would adjust the course along the way, as things seldom go as planned. Leadership, change, sustainable growth, and development fluctuate.

The more difficult it was to reach the desired results, the more I learned and the stronger and more resilient I became. Especially when I worked as president for the North American organization, there were long periods when the United States was going through a very unstable economic cycle. We had opened so many new stores with different sales results and performance levels that it made the internal numbers difficult to predict. This experience taught me to hang tight through the hard times. You learn more about your own leadership in difficult times than when things are going well. You need to trust that you are on track and that it is all part of the journey. Success and good ideas often come out of challenging times.

I constantly have conversations with my kids around who they are and what is important to them. We talk about a general direction and how they want to live their lives. As they are now both in their early twenties, they are experiencing every day that, as much as they have a general direction, life throws them curve balls constantly and they have to adjust.

This brings me to the compass. For me, it is the perfect alternative to a career plan.

TOOL

FIND YOUR PASSION

Passion is really about connecting with your own natural source of energy. If you have lost connection over the years or don't know really what it is that gives you energy, you will need to ask yourself a lot of questions and be willing to try something new. (This practice is inspired by the book *The Artist's Way* by Julia Cameron.)

1. Do something out of the ordinary one day a week. Spend time alone, visit a museum, see a movie in the middle of the day, take a walk in the woods, take some photographs, or start practicing yoga. It will open you up to new experiences and make you realize that small adjustments in your everyday life can bring more joy and happiness.

2. Look back on your childhood, recall some special moments, write them down, and describe why they were special. This will give you insights into what gets you excited and brings you joy. If joy is missing in your life today, then ask yourself how you can use this new discovery to add more excitement. Take a good look at whether anything is holding you back.

3. Ask yourself more questions: What is truly important to you? Do you love what you are doing? What is it that gives you energy? When are you the happiest? What truly matters to you? What does not? What will you do more of? What will you do less of?

4. Write a letter to yourself from the vantage point of five years into the future. Describe the life you are living. How are you feeling about yourself? Describe the people in your life. Whom do

you love and where are you living? What are you doing? What matters to you? What are you engaged in?

5. To reconnect to or discover your passion doesn't mean you will be doing passionate things 24/7. It might mean just to add more things into your life that bring you joy and happiness.

5

THE POWERFUL COMPASS

When my daughter was eighteen years old and in the process of applying to college, I sat down and talked with her about the future. I remembered how in my own life when I was her age, I was almost in a panic because I needed answers about what I wanted to study and what type of work I would like to do long-term.

It is overwhelming having to make all sorts of plans for the future at such a young age, and here in the United States, there is additional pressure to get into a "good university." I have told my children that they need to see that time as the beginning of their adulthood. It is a time to find out who you are and what you want. It is okay to be in doubt.

It was important for me to talk to my daughter about how to use her personal compass rather than which major would be the "right" one. A compass is an instrument for determining who you are and what you want out of your life. In my career, it has been more about living my mission in life than about reaching a particular goal. Along the way, I have used the compass. My values, my passion, my strength, and my personal well-being function as its four cardinal points. They have helped me navigate and find my way when I have gone off course.

Now I didn't very consciously set my course when I was eighteen, but by the time I was in my early twenties, I had an idea that I was adventurous and was fascinated by other cultures, people, leadership, and design. Thinking back to that time, I would certainly have benefitted from having someone I trusted to talk to about my desires and dreams for the future. The earlier you realize what you're passionate about, the greater the chance that you will create a life where your passion is an integral, natural part of everything you do.

Today, the compass is a very important tool for me, and my conversations with my children always stress its value. In one of my daughter's college applications, she had to answer the question "Who are you?" For me that's the essence of life. When you find out who you are and what is important to you, you are better equipped to manage your life and make decisions. You have a unique opportunity to think about how you want to live your life. What will the journey look like?

For my daughter, it was a new idea, but for me, it was also an aha moment, and it struck me that we all have the opportunity to take ourselves, our lives, and our situations and review them on a regular basis. Instead of just letting things happen, we can first ask ourselves what kind of life we want. What is important to us? What is our personal mission? When we answer these questions, then we can clarify what our values, our passions, and our strengths are, really getting down to the core of what is important for our well-being. By describing it broadly, rather than getting specific and narrow, you have your compass. Every time we are confronted with an offer or a choice, we can ask ourselves if it will lead in the direction we want.

The answer will sometimes be no. This does not necessarily mean that you need to say no to a task or job. Maybe it's okay for your career to spend a few years taking a detour, but if you have clarity about your overall mission, you can make that choice much more consciously. If you have a clear idea about where you are heading, it is easier to get back on track again.

Starting college is, for most young adults, a stressful time. Every aspect of it—being away from home, dorm life, finding friends, surviving academically, fitting in, and the list goes on. For some, joining a sorority or fraternity is the answer. My daughter had not yet found a good group of friends in her first semester, and she was not sure if joining a sorority was what she was looking for.

She is social and outgoing, but she didn't know enough about sororities as networks to rule them out, so she went through the rush process and was accepted but ended up saying no. She was interested in being part of a group and finding friends she could relate to, but she felt a sorority was not the answer for her. She was relieved on one hand once she made a decision, but she was also frustrated about still not being part of a group. She continued to search, and followed her interest and passion for social justice and community involvement, and she soon realized the school had many groups with service and community work as a focus. She joined two organizations and moved into a dorm specifically for these students. She used her passion and values to make the right choice for her.

We all find ourselves in similar situations when we are unclear about what to do. We have to stay open, allow ourselves to be confused as we research the options, maybe even trying something new before we come to the right decision. Although being part of a sorority was ultimately contrary to my daughter's interests, it was important and clarifying for her to examine the possibility. She was aware of why she wanted to go through the process, and her initial feeling was confirmed in the end. The whole process is an example of how the compass can guide us on both what not to do and what new direction we want to move in.

If we are conscious about what we do, it's also okay if the result is different from what we had hoped for. Even when we are completely clear on what matters most to us, we can still be in doubt in a certain situation and find ourselves pushed in a different direction. Therefore, it is important that you remember to stick to your personal compass and ask yourself: Will this lead me in the direction I want to go? Is this in alignment with my core values?

Let's say you feel that something new needs to happen in your job. Encouragement from both colleagues and your boss has led you to consider becoming a manager. In some ways, you have always felt that it would be exciting to have more influence and make decisions, but on the other hand, you are not so keen on pressure and having the ultimate responsibility. So you step out of your comfort zone and participate in a management seminar. Stepping away from your job for a few days and exploring more about management roles will give you clarity. Whatever decision you make will be right because you took responsibility for your situation, and took the time to reflect and find out more about what a management role entails. I have met many specialists who know that they don't want to take on management responsibilities; they like their role, don't have any interest in the increased responsibility, and would most likely not be good managers. I have also seen many great specialists who had a wish to grow and take on more responsibility, and they have become excellent managers. When others ask, "Am I a born leader?" I always ask, "Do you want to be a leader?" For me, it is a matter of deciding for ourselves.

Regardless of whether you are a young, uncertain student or have tons of experience in the working world, your compass can be a huge help, a lifeline when you have to make a choice. You have something to hold on to when the ride becomes bumpy and overwhelming, or if you are in doubt about whether you are doing the right thing.

INVEST TIME TO FIND YOUR MISSION

I am very mission driven and always need to know the *why*. IKEA is a mission-driven company and part of why I loved working for the company for so long. It wasn't about just selling furniture; the company mission—"creating a better life for many people"—is what I wanted to contribute to. A personal mission is just as important, and I have found great inspiration in the book *The Alchemist* by Paulo Coelho. One of Coelho's main points is that our most important responsibility here on earth is to find out what we are here to do, to find our personal legend.

For most of us, it is quite difficult to describe what we are here to do, what we really burn for, what we will leave behind. In my own family, among friends, and with colleagues, there is such a difference from person to person. I remember walking along the beach a few years back, asking my husband about his personal legend, as I had spent a few days thinking about my own. He was quite clear: "It is to be the best possible father to our kids and to have influence on the kids I come in contact with through my work as an educator." It was clear to him. He turned to me and asked, "What about yours?"

Hearing the question asked so directly, I suddenly realized that I didn't have a clear answer and it encouraged my personal work to find my mission. I always knew that it was something about seeing people grow. Today I have formulated my mission. Keep in mind that it is a work in progress: "When I am grounded in who I am, empowered by my unlimited potential, and take leadership for creating the life I want to live, I will give energy and power to others. Together we will impact the people and the world around us."

I recently mentored a fantastic, young, talented, ambitious woman, and when we had our first meeting, she shared with me that her biggest goal was to get a management position with her company. One of my first questions to her was what she wanted with her life. It took a while for her to move from the focus on the immediate goal to the much broader question about her mission in life. This process initiated lots of additional thoughts about her personal life, career, and passion. Months later, when she had created her mission, she no longer felt an urgency to become a manager, and she had discovered a few different opportunities and options for what she wanted next.

As my son was applying for college, we spent time together clarifying his long-term mission. When you are seventeen, that's an overwhelming question, but I didn't give up. "Try to describe what is important to you. Where do you see yourself heading? How will you spend the next few years developing yourself as a person with that in mind?" I asked him.

At the time, he got my point but listened halfheartedly and was not ready to get into much of a discussion and take it seriously. Preparing to go to college, he just wanted to find a good subject for his essay and get it out of the way. He had been inspired by his dad for years and had decided he wanted to be an elementary school teacher, so he wrote an essay about his motivation being the lack of male teachers in those early years of education.

The discussions with my son have been ongoing now for a couple years, and he is much more aware and clear about what he wants in his life, what his values are, and why he really wants to be a teacher. He didn't have the best experience in elementary school himself; he connected with only two teachers and, for the most part, lacked the joy for learning during these formative years. He has experienced, on a personal level, the impact teachers have on children's interest in learning from an early age and for the rest of their lives. At one point during college, he took a semester off school, as he was just not motivated to study. He worked for five months at an elementary school as a recess coach, and the connection with the kids in first and second grade made him truly connect with why he wanted to be a teacher.

You can use the same method of clarification, regardless of your age or the nature of the problem you are facing. Maybe you are forty-three years old and in a period where you aren't really clear about what you want and need. Perhaps the passion and motivation are gone, and you can't see the horizon. It is time to ask yourself the big questions: What is important to me? How would I like to see my life in three to four years? What do I want to do in the future? What really interests me? When am I most happy?

Connect back to a special moment in your life when you felt really happy. How can you get more of that feeling? What has meaning for you and what doesn't? Is there something you would like to do more of? What would you like to do less of? If you focus on something that has meant something special to you, you can get a sense of what really interests you and turns you on. But you will have to invest time to figure it out. It doesn't just pop up on its own.

For some people, it is a completely natural and fluid process that is going on all the time. Unfortunately, it is not like that for most of us. The good news is that the time and patience you invest in finding the answers can come back tenfold and genuinely transform the way you live your life. Beware of the urge to find a quick solution and the even greater temptation of doing nothing. The easy way out is to live a life where the days just pass by. I have often heard people say, "Yes, but things are good for me. I might have some days that are less good than others, but on the whole I am doing okay." Maybe it's time to ask yourself if okay is truly good enough.

TREAT YOURSELF TO A TIME-OUT

If we really want change, we have to make the decision to do something. Stop and take a time-out. Either we decide to take one or it will happen unplanned, triggered by getting fired, childbirth, stress, or an illness.

You've probably had lots of conversations with your friends about your desire for change. I know I have. One of my friends was having a hard time with her job, but when it came right down to it, she was not interested in making any radical changes. She wasn't interested in being a supervisor or manager, or in changing jobs to create renewed energy. But she was having a hard time, and something had to happen. Who hasn't been in a situation like this, where you spend a lot of time and effort complaining about work or other things that can't be solved? Her solution came down to "Let it be as it is," and she began to focus on her life outside of work. She freed up a lot of energy by no longer spending so much of it being dissatisfied over things she wasn't going to do anything about. Even without changing jobs, she did something very powerful by making a conscious decision.

In such situations, you have three options: you can choose to accept the state of things, try to change them, or leave the job. Each of the three solutions is perfectly fine. The solution that's right all depends on who you are as a person and your ambitions. I probably wouldn't have made the same choice she did, but it was a fine solution for her. We are all different. What matters is that you choose the option that suits you and where you are in your life at that moment.

Another of my friends felt that she had lost the passion in her life, that she had been living for other people. She worked hard at her job and tried to be there 100 percent for her children. In other words, she had fallen into the routine of managing her job and caring for her family, and had let all her own needs and talents slip more and more into the background.

She needed to take a step back, put herself on the agenda, take a time-out, and ask, "Am I going in the right direction?"

Once you have given yourself a break a few times, you can start to make it a habit. When you start to feel you have no control over the direction your life is taking, you automatically stop and reflect. If taking a break is new to you, it can easily take six months to a year to arrive at something resembling a solution. But remember that the process is extremely valuable and that you can get something really good out of it.

This doesn't mean you need to take a year off. I see it more as a very conscious decision to stop and reflect and make time for yourself and the process you need to go through to possibly change course. Use a mentor, a therapist, and your friends, and keep a journal. Take the time to look at what you want out of your life. Make time to think about how you can have more control over your life, so you can prioritize the things you really enjoy instead of letting things get away from you.

The problem is that we often end up concentrating on the difficult issues when we are most frustrated and do not feel that we have resources.

What happens when you say, "I am tired of my bedroom. Something has to change"? I bet you will invest money and time in the project. You make a plan for a new room and select colors, furniture, textiles, and lighting. You can make the same kind of decision with respect to yourself and your own life. I know from experience that it's not easy, especially when you are worn-out mentally, but take yourself and your irritation or frustration seriously. Find out what you want to change and how to do it.

When it comes to personal development and to looking critically and constructively at one's own life, which is much more important than having the perfect bedroom, there is no simple checklist. You may not feel that you have the necessary tools, and it can feel a bit awkward to sit and talk about how important it is to make a plan. But could there be anything more important? We all have to take responsibility, just as we do when we want a nicer home with a comfortable, beautiful bedroom.

Personal feelings are, of course, more complicated than selecting wall colors, mattresses, and bed frames, and you can't make a plan that fits everyone. It is also not common to have a personal life plan, whereas it is quite normal to have a fitness plan and a career plan. It is perfectly okay to hire a personal trainer to help you get fit, or a contractor to help you renovate your kitchen, but it is not quite as common to get someone to help you get your personal life on track. However, without a plan, you cannot expect real change.

SMALL STEPS

The problem with many plans is that they are often so radical that they end up being useless. It is tempting to set really high goals and a fast timeline for ourselves, so we can see results fast. It's always motivating to get started, but in reality, the too ambitious, rigorous plan is hard to implement and follow through on.

It's easier to commit to smaller, manageable plans, and make smaller adjustments that can more easily become habits and are then naturally integrated into your life.

The challenge for many of us is to get started. One way is to immerse ourselves in a specific program for a period of time. This could be a month-long yoga program or an intensive three-week personal development retreat—but for many people with busy lives and limited financial resources, it can be hard to invest both the money and time.

When I was on vacation not so long ago, I decided to follow a program outlined in a book called *The 21-Day Consciousness Cleanse: A Breakthrough Program for Connecting with Your Soul's Deepest Purpose,* by Debbie Ford. It fit perfectly with my three-week vacation, was very spiritual, and dealt precisely with how you want to live your life. It was twenty-one days of exercises to be done every day. It was hard work, lots of reflection and writing, and there were a couple days I skipped—but sticking to it for a period of time helped me refocus some areas of my life and come back from vacation with some new insights about myself.

Over time, most of us have learned that we can't change eating and exercise habits by snapping a finger. In too many cases, we end up falling back into old routines as we allow our plans to slide, or we become fanatics and lose the rest of our lives as we attempt to maintain the standards. If we want sustainable changes, it requires a shift in our minds and consciousness about the way we live our everyday life. It's like a kaleidoscope; by shifting just slightly, something new appears, we see new possibilities, and we realize just small changes can make a big difference in our everyday lives.

THE POWER OF PATIENCE

Be realistic and patient. Forget the idea that life changes radically from one day to the next. However, I want to inspire you to continually prioritize your time for yourself and your life. When you are in the process of internally "redecorating" your life, make some simple exercises that can remove barriers that, at the moment, are preventing you from living the life you want to lead.

If you are online all the time and not mentally present, take a day when you turn your smartphone and computer off. You can also decide to write fewer text messages. Keep an email-free weekend. Check your Facebook, Twitter, or Instagram account only once a day.

It is important to get new habits integrated into your consciousness. I have often wondered why it is so difficult to meditate for five or ten minutes every day. On paper it doesn't sound like much, but it's hard because we have jobs and we want to work out, care for and spend time with our children, cook for them, and then keep everything else running smoothly.

I work on setting realistic goals for myself, and I test them in a conversation with someone I trust. Today my compass is in hand for both small and big things, and my journal is one of the most important tools I have.

I first learned to keep a journal when I was in the midst of a difficult time. I followed some tips and practices from the book *The Artist's Way*, which aims to help artists with creative blocks. The good thing about keeping a journal is that it forces you to dive a little deeper into yourself. When I read what I have written, there is generally a pattern or some explanations that become apparent, revealing why I am doing well or why I am not.

Writing a journal is good for me. Sometimes I write every day, and other times once a month. It all depends on where I am in my life. Writing helps me figure out where things aren't working, what I am happy about, and what I want to focus on. Getting my ideas, intentions, and thoughts down on paper has a great effect and gets me motivated to make the necessary changes. Although I do not look in the diary every day, it always amazes me when I look back and read what I wrote a few months ago, how most of the time the things I said I wanted to focus on actually happened. It gives me confidence and motivation to continue to use my journal.

It is my best friend.

I am not talking about huge, ambitious projects. It might be that in the next six months, I will stop procrastinating and take care of practical tasks that have piled up, I will focus on having friends over for dinner and stay in closer contact with my sisters. A very specific example was getting my Illinois driver's license when we moved to Chicago. I had been ignoring it for way too long and didn't get it done until I had put in my journal that I wanted to take care of my practical duties.

As CEO for IKEA North America, writing down my intentions for the next few months was so important in keeping me focused and addressing the most critical topics. You can do the same. Write down the big things you want to accomplish. You don't have to maniacally focus on the selected projects. You can simply write them down and keep them in the back of your mind. The power of writing something down on paper makes you more conscious, and for me it worked—I got it done.

HOW TO ADJUST YOUR JOB COMPASS

All the earlier examples in the book have been about adjusting your compass in small but effective ways. The really big effects come when you use your compass to make big decisions. If you have ambitions of taking on a big leadership position, you need to consider if there are things you really like in your current job that you will have to give up, and if there will be enough excitement in the new job to make up for the loss. I have seen many people get burned-out and stressed because they have moved away from what they really enjoyed and truly loved for a new title and more money.

In my own career, my job as a store manager was in many ways my best job. When I agreed to take the position as HR manager for IKEA North America in 1997, it was my passion for making a difference for my hourly coworkers in the stores and unleashing the potential of our people that excited me. When I said yes to becoming president of IKEA North America in 2001, it was based on my passion for leadership, development, and change.

When I got the top job, I used the compass in a new way. It soon became clear to me that I had to find a way to handle the pressure. It wasn't just that I was confronted with large, new challenges, but I also had more focus on me as a person. My primary task was to strengthen IKEA's position in the North American market, especially in the United States, where the population was hardly aware of IKEA. The main priority was to expand by twenty-six new stores by 2010. It had taken us over twenty years to build twenty-four stores, so more than doubling our size in half the time was a huge operation. To further strengthen our position, we also moved a large number of existing stores to better locations and rebuilt small stores to full-size concept stores. In addition, we needed to integrate the North American regional setup into a global setup, which was huge in itself.

It was exciting and challenging but also a massive responsibility, and I could have easily taken on the problems twenty-four hours a day. The changes created lots of questions from our employees, many critical decisions had to be made every day, and dissatisfied customers never disappear in the retail industry. The scope of the job would have absorbed me 100 percent, seven days a week, if I hadn't realized that I had to set boundaries to keep perspective and not lose myself. I had to adjust my job compass. Among other things, I decided to go home by 5:30 whenever I was not away on business. It was a very simple and effective way to set my own boundaries and give my brain room to breathe. Employees could also be absolutely sure that I wouldn't call or email them on weekends unless there was an urgent issue. I knew my behavior sent an important message to the employees; they were not expected to work at every possible and impossible moment either.

Here in the United States, we work a lot. It is not unusual to work sixty to seventy hours a week, but this doesn't mean we are effective during all those hours. For me it was a question of being a good example, for others and for myself. It was important to stick to my principles in order to work effectively, but also to let others take responsibility, letting me prioritize my time so I could recharge at home with family.

If I had not set some ground rules that took my own well-being into account, I would not have been able to do my job well. Experience has taught me that if I do not follow my own compass, I can easily lose myself.

TOOL

DESCRIBE YOUR PERSONAL MISSION

A personal mission statement provides clarity and gives us a sense of purpose. It defines who we are, how we live our lives, and what we are here to do, accomplish, and leave behind. It is short, to the point, and can guide you on your life journey. It might sound difficult to capture, but a simple way to get started is to consider what you want to be remembered for when you are no longer here.

1. What mission are you on? What impact do you want to have and on whom? This is not about creating peace in the world. Keep it to something you can control.
2. Through which core values will your carry out your life mission? What are the personal behaviors you will live by?
3. Write your answers out with words that inspire and guide you.
4. If this is your very first time even thinking about a mission statement for your life, remember: don't overthink it. Get started with something and keep developing it over time as you become clearer. It is not a project done in a day. Give yourself time.
5. Include a friend, partner, family member, or colleague in your creative process. It can be a fun thing to do together.

6

VALUES—THE MOST IMPORTANT TOOL

I love living in the States. When I left Denmark in the 1980s, it wasn't my plan to be here for the rest of my life. But I have always been fascinated by the US sense of freedom and that there is so much room for people to be themselves. If you do well, others celebrate. There is a spirit of celebrating others' success. It is quite different from Denmark, where success often triggers envy and jealousy.

The lifestyle and values in the United States fit my family and me well. It was my brother who first moved to the United States, and then I followed. Not long after, my parents and my little sister came, and finally my oldest sister. Maybe it is in our DNA, because my great-grandparents on my father's side immigrated to the States but left their son, my grandfather, behind in Denmark. Although I am now a US citizen, it was important for me to work in a Scandinavian company, where humanistic values are at the core of the business. Those are the values I grew up with, and they are important to me.

Leadership at IKEA is based on values. When I attended a leadership seminar some years ago, I was asked to write a list of my own personal values, and it became very clear to me how important they are as part of your compass.

I can't emphasize strongly enough how big of an impact putting my four key values into words has had, and I highly recommend you do the same. Often confusion and discontent come from our values not aligning with our company, our boss, or maybe even a partner or friend.

If I look around at my professional network and my friends and family, I see many who have aspirations to do something different, but they are not prepared to do what it takes. There are certainly many explanations for why it is so difficult. If you can't quite figure out how to move forward and get beyond the feeling of being discontent, you might be low on confidence or are perhaps not really clear on what you want.

I have met many people, especially women, who are stuck in denial and frustration. I hope to inspire people to change that kind of thinking from "this is what I don't like" to "what do I want?" Discovering and clarifying our own values is an incredible practice and guide in all aspects of life. We all have at least a few values that seem to be built in; others come from our upbringing, and some we have developed through life.

When I attended that same leadership seminar at IKEA, I became aware of how extremely important values are for me. If I am unhappy in a certain situation or a job, it is usually because my work is not aligned with my personal values.

There are probably psychological explanations of how our values control many of our actions in a specific direction, but to put it simply, formulating my fundamental values gave me great personal insight. Things become much more clear, whether you are seeking the right job or work in a company that is aligned with who you are.

MATCHING VALUES

IKEA's culture and business are based on very clear and strong values of cost consciousness, simplicity, moving forward, the courage to think differently, humility, leadership by example, acceptance, and responsibility. The company is down-to-earth, Scandinavian, and Swedish in its values. Its culture is one that is relevant everywhere. The values are basic human values, and they exist in most cultures and countries, which is why IKEA can exist and be successful all over the world, and have a culture that can thrive in Pittsburgh, Shanghai, Rome, and Malmo.

Values are a big part of any company's success, and it goes without saying that if you want to work for IKEA, you will not succeed if you don't have similar values. For me personally, it was always a great opportunity and very rewarding to be an ambassador for those values and more in North America. They were a major reason I worked for IKEA for twenty-one years.

Had I been primarily motivated by money and prestige, IKEA would not have been right. Money is important to me, but it not a key driver. Of course IKEA pays well and is competitive to attract good people. The compensation system is quite transparent and well communicated to the employees. But if you join IKEA thinking you will become a billionaire, drive an expensive company car, and fly in business class, you have chosen the wrong place. I have met candidates who were impressed by the values and wanted to benefit from IKEA's culture but had no desire to actually live it.

Humbleness is one of the core values of IKEA, and was also a value I grew up with in Denmark. The downside of humbleness, at least in Denmark, is that you do not feel special and extraordinary—but the positive side of humbleness is not taking oneself too seriously and not believing we are better than anyone else.

As I was preparing for a keynote speech in Long Beach, California, for eight hundred female entrepreneurs, I listened to Norah Jones's song "Humble Me," and it became the theme of my speech—I discussed different situations in my life that had humbled me.

I had just returned from vacation, and the whole family had come together to be with my father, who was suffering from an aggressive form of cancer that killed him within six months. That humbled me.

Another example is when I started my job and was responsible for IKEA in North America. I was determined to change the leadership culture and IKEA's external image by having more female managers and introducing greater ethnic diversity. Over 70 percent of IKEA's customers are women, and many markets have a large ethnically diverse population and customer base, and as IKEA had too few customers and too narrow of an existing customer base, it was important to develop both the business and the people. It was also a natural continuation of the global HR strategy, which I had helped to develop as HR manager for IKEA North America. After the first three years, I could see a lot of progress, but we had also made some unfortunate mistakes and taken some steps backward. The recognition that truly sustainable changes on such a value-loaded issue take time humbled me.

MY FOUR CORE VALUES

As a leader, I have to be myself and show employees what I stand for and what is important to me. It makes me honest and transparent, and people will understand who I am and what my message is, whether they agree with it or not. That is the leadership philosophy at IKEA and one I have come to embrace.

It requires us to constantly develop as people and in our roles. For instance, I constantly ask myself: Who am I as a leader? But in fact, the question may just as well be: Who am I as a person? It is a question worth asking. The first step I went through to find the answer was to go back to my childhood and look at what was important to me and to my family. I did the same for the other stages of my life. I asked: What has had the greatest meaning?

By asking myself these sorts of questions, I have found out that commitment and loyalty are the values that hold it all together for me. They are not really my own; they came from my upbringing, and they are a sense of security for me.

My own values are passion, courage, and trust. When something connects with these values, I feel tremendously committed and engaged.

I have to love what I do; I have to have passion. My energy level, my enthusiasm, and my leadership are unbelievably important for me. I discover possibilities everywhere, in people and in every task. I am passionate about leading, transformation, new ideas, and being part of unleashing the potential of people—especially the ones who, by no choice of their own, are facing some difficult barriers. I care deeply about diversity, social issues, and social justice, just as I love the home furnishings business and entrepreneurship.

Courage is important to me. As a leader, I must dare to stand up and embrace my imperfections, my mistakes, and the fact that I do not have all the answers. I must stand for something and have a clear point of view. I need courage to be unpopular and to tolerate negative feedback, critique, and being seen. If I can't manage a little discomfort, I can't get anything done. For me, things that are worthwhile are often also quite difficult and take courage. I love to try new things and need the courage to change the status quo.

Trust is another core value. It connects back to my childhood, when my parents always showed unconditional trust in me. I was allowed to go out late at night and to travel alone at a very early age. My parents have never given me anything but 100 percent trust, and I don't think they feel I ever broke it. It has been such a gift in my life, and I want to pay it forward.

My children, my husband, my family, and my friends have my trust, but I also trust people in general. If you work for me, you don't have to earn my trust. You get it automatically, and it is up to you to manage it. Some say I'm too trusting and almost naïve, but I am rarely disappointed. If you feel confident, you are also more motivated, and you feel confident when you know you have your boss's trust.

Commitment is an inherited value of mine that characterized my upbringing and my personality to a large degree. I see it as part of my fundamental identity. Commitment and loyalty will always lie deep within me.

I feel a strong sense of loyalty toward everything I say yes to. I will continue to work on whatever it is until it succeeds. In this context, I have often given people many chances, and it has sometimes happened that they give up before I do. With my family, my bosses, and my friends, I am likewise extremely loyal and committed. It is my strength but also my weakness. As always, there are the two extremes. I have often defended people when others around me have been scratching their heads. If I decide to do something with someone, then that person can count on me and my support 100 percent. I move forward as we have agreed until, together, we decide otherwise.

THE RIGHT MATCH

My professional values aren't different from my personal values. Integration of who you are at work and at home is important and necessary for your health. In one context or another, we all put on certain personas in business, but I don't think that being split between the two personas is sustainable over time.

As my kids have gotten older, I have had conversations with them about their values. For my son, independence is important, and for my daughter, social justice is, so as they look ahead, knowing this can help them in aligning their personal and professional lives.

Here's what I know about the importance of values: I need to have a job that I feel good about working at. The company's values and work culture must match what I believe in. And even though I seek to make a difference and be a leader, I also have to be interested and excited about the business itself. The company's mission needs to inspire me, and I need to be interested in its product and output. The work environment must also present possibilities for me to explore new ideas, and new ways of thinking must be encouraged.

I'm sure you will find that unhappiness and discontent, both at work and in your life, are often caused by a mismatch between your personal values and your company's values.

If you are a person who values freedom, you aren't likely to enjoy working at a place where you have to meet at 8 AM sharp each day and punch a clock. If you are happy being independent and taking responsibility, it is likely going to be frustrating to have a boss who stands over you constantly checking your work.

If one of your core values is social responsibility and you are concerned about social justice and ethics, then working for a company that uses child labor would be a problem. You can surely come up with other good examples. Maybe you have sometimes wondered how you get along so well with a person who has interests that are very different from yours. My guess is that your chemistry is related to the fact that you share many of the same values in life.

As a new mother, thinking about and reflecting on values comes naturally. Mothers quickly decide the values they want their children to grow up with. They may not write them down on paper, but they know they will teach their children to always tell the truth and treat others with respect.

When we start a family, get married, or have a new love in our life, it also becomes clear how important it is to know our own values as well as our partner's. Problems in relationships arise often because the two people do not have the same values, or do not respect or understand each other's values. If the relationship is based on both collective and individual values, it is usually easier to stop and adjust when you run into a rough patch—just as you can personally use your values to check when you are not feeling okay.

UNCOVER YOUR VALUES

When you are ready to articulate your values, it is important to be honest with yourself. You can begin by writing a long list of things that matter to you. Then you have to boil it down and prioritize what is most important so the list can be used easily for future reference.

In the process of finding your values, you may realize you live by some values that you unconsciously have inherited from childhood. Now is the chance to consciously choose which ones you want to keep going forward. It's time to let go of the ones that don't serve you anymore. A sense of duty is a classic. It may be important, but perhaps it is one of the values that you must free yourself from and scratch off the list.

For the most part, our basic values remain consistent. They are a part of our DNA, but their meaning can change over time, and new values can emerge. What matters is that you dare to be honest with yourself. There are certain values so deeply ingrained that you can't get rid of them. They are a part of you, whether you like it or not, and you usually don't choose or develop them yourself.

If you are like me, your gut is the best way to know if you are living according to your values. If something doesn't feel right, there is clearly a conflict somewhere. Today I am pretty good at sensing when I have compromised my values. I can feel a strong sense of discomfort and unease in my gut. The opposite is true as well.

TOOL

FIND YOUR CORE VALUES

Core values are typically defined as the fundamental beliefs of a person, the guiding principles that dictate behavior and action, and they can help a person know what is right or wrong. They create an unwavering and unchanging guide.

1. Look back on your life until now, including your childhood. What values did you grow up with? What things were important to you as a child? What values are you living today?

2. When you have a total of about thirty values, begin to edit them down. Many are likely a subconscious part of your growth and development. You need to question the values. Are dutifulness and being on time important values for you? Or do you live according to them because you carried them with you from childhood?

3. When you have about fifteen values on your list, look at yourself as a person today. What values are most important to you? What values are an inseparable part of you as a person? What values can you wave good-bye to because they no longer serve you?

4. See if you can narrow the fifteen down to about five by prioritizing them. See if some overlap, like honesty, trust, integrity, so you can combine them into one word.

5. Ask a family member, a good friend, or colleague if they are willing to participate. Share your core values with this person and discuss why these specifically matter to you. Share the process you went through. Get feedback to determine if you behave

according to your values and if there is something important you are missing. It's good to get different perspectives, so you can get as close to the real you as possible.

6. Come to a conclusion. Decide on four to six values. Write them down and start relying on these in all parts of your life. They work very well as a part of your compass.

EXAMPLES OF CORE VALUES

Dependable, reliable, loyal, committed, open-minded, consistent, honest, efficient, innovative, creative, humorous, fun loving, adventurous, motivated, positive, optimistic, inspiring, passionate, respectful, fit, fair, courageous, educated, curious, loving, trusted.

7

FIND YOUR AUTHENTIC SELF

Living in the United States, I have always felt that I could be myself. When I moved here, right from the start, I was met with enormous acceptance. It was a new feeling for me. In Denmark, I had felt more constrained. In the Danish culture, there are strict unwritten rules about what one should and can do. As much as it is one of the most accepting places, safe, and very democratic, there is an underlying culture of conformity, one that asks that you not stick out too much and by no means ever think you are anything special. In addition, I also grew up in a very small community. Moving from Copenhagen in first grade to a small rural village wasn't easy. It took a long time to be accepted, and I felt like I was living in a costume for many years.

For much of my childhood, I felt that I couldn't be myself. I can imagine that I share this feeling with many who grew up in similar communities. Fortunately, I met my best friend, and we are still best friends today. She helped me feel safe; she saw who I really was and helped me dare to be myself. She liked me for who I was. Once, at the beginning of our friendship, I made fun of her to impress one of the popular girls. I remember her starting to cry and running to the bathroom. I went after her and was met with, "Why can't you just be yourself?"

I had been cruel to my best friend to be popular and accepted, and it was quite mature and impressive for her at the age of ten to recognize that I was not being myself. My immigration attorney said something similar when he helped me get my paperwork done to settle in the United States: "Don't ever compare yourself to others. If you constantly compare yourself to others, you will be lost."

I completely agree, but we do not have to move away from our homeland to get in touch with our authentic self. I got nothing for free by moving. I simply got a new start. No one knew me or had preconceived ideas about me. But right away I could just tell that there was space for me as a person. I could be myself and felt more confident than I had in Denmark. I no longer felt any pressure that I had to play a role or do certain things. It is quite possible that I had created the pressure in my own head, but who has that kind of insight at twenty-three? I certainly didn't.

My move triggered a combination of things that made me feel free. With that said, I am aware that I also put my life on autopilot for several years while I concentrated on work, having children, starting different jobs, and getting into a rhythm, and time and my life just went by. During that kind of a phase, it can be hard to stop and take a good look at who you are—and what you really dream about. There have been periods when I believed that I could handle more than what was realistic, but I can say for sure that I never imagined or tried to be anyone other than myself—not since that day long ago when I let down my best friend.

BE YOUR OWN ROLE MODEL

I have often been asked who my role models are. I never had a good answer, and later I understood why. For many years, I felt a pressure to name a few, but there are so many amazing people I admire. At some point, I realized I actually don't believe in the concept of having a role model. Many people have inspired me, taught me things, or have done something that impressed me. Inspiring people are all around us, but I never wished I were like Mother Teresa, Madeleine Albright, Meryl Streep, or Oprah. I don't get jealous and frustrated because I am not as smart, famous, good-looking, or accomplished as someone else. Of course it has entered my thoughts at times that I might not be as good, but it has never pushed me in the direction of wanting to be like someone else.

I look at Oprah, for example, with eagerness to see what it is about her that interests me: What capabilities does she have that I can learn from? Is there something about her way of being that I can use to learn more about who I am as a person?

It's a way of thinking that has been with me since arriving in the United States. The time I worked for Stor in California was a good example of how copying is not a viable option.

The company had simply tried to copy IKEA's furniture and concept, and was sued by IKEA. As a Stor employee, I experienced what takes place when there is only a plan A, which was to be just like IKEA and have just as much success. The problem was that when things did not go as expected, no one knew what needed to be done. Plan B did not exist. No one in the company knew the fundamental, underlying structure and concept of IKEA.

In my opinion, it is exactly the same thing that happens if I want to be like someone else. If I let go of my responsibility and say, "Show me the way," it doesn't work, because you can't take over someone else's motivation and mind-set. You have to start with yourself.

Many feel like sports stars should be role models, but for me it is enough that they are simply good examples, and that we can all be too. You can set a good example as a leader, friend, and person by being confident and authentic. The term *role model* I associate with perfection. If you put someone on a pedestal and give them the status of role model, you are looking for perfection outside yourself and distancing yourself from ownership and responsibility.

WHO AM I?

Surely "Who am I?" is one of the biggest questions we can ask ourselves. The answer becomes clearer as we grow as individuals. Even though insight often comes with age, it is not a given. Statistics can't predict when you will arrive at this deeper insight.

Maybe you are very young and already radiating a solid and rooted sense of yourself. Maybe you are well into your forties and still haven't quite dared to step into who you are. You must, in other words, still make an effort to find your authentic self. The first step is to come to grips with the fear of being who you are.

One of my favorite quotes illustrates this very well. In *The Dance*, Oriah Mountain Dreamer asks, "What if the question is not why am I so infrequently the person I really want to be, but why do I so infrequently want to be the person I really am?" Yes, why are we so afraid to be ourselves at full blast? Instead of giving yourself a completely impossible task by thinking that you should be like someone you know or have read about, why not ask yourself, "Why not just be who I am? Why is it that I do not want to be that person?" If you are working on finding out who you are and focusing on yourself, instead of always being concerned with what others are doing, you are on the path toward your authentic self.

I have read several books on the subject. *The Shadow Effect* by Debbie Ford, Deepak Chopra, and Marianne Williamson reaches back to childhood and examines how we all have light and darkness. If you do not recognize your dark side, you will automatically see less light. This is not because we are all born bad people, but because we must face the fact that we have both and need to embrace both. The two sides are a combination of education and experience, and slowly developed as we got older.

When we are born, we are our most authentic self, but soon our mother begins to say what we should eat, maybe even if we are not hungry. Both in school and at home, we are told what we may and may not do. We adapt to our culture, to the rules that are set before us. For years, we are influenced by opinions, religions, and expectations, and over time, this has great impact on how we see the world and ourselves. Our world is created by a number of both internal and external experiences and is far from who we initially were as a newborn human being.

The Four Agreements by don Miguel Ruiz also challenged and guided me to get closer to my core self, the essence of me. It suggests:

1. **Be impeccable with your words.** Speak with integrity; say only what you really mean.
2. **Don't take anything personally.** Nothing others do is because of you.
3. **Don't make assumptions.** Find the courage to ask questions and to express what you really want.
4. **Always do your best.** Under all circumstances, do your best, and you will avoid self-judgment, self-abuse, and regret.

DON'T LIE TO YOURSELF

Honesty applies to the smallest everyday interactions. A friend invites you to dinner and asks if you like lamb. She and her husband found this incredible recipe and they want to share a special meal with you. You don't like lamb and choose to be honest and say, "No, unfortunately, I don't like lamb." You do not disappoint. On the contrary, you reward your good friend with honesty—and yourself too.

Of course, there are times when it is hard to be completely honest. Let's imagine that you are visiting your elderly grandmother, who has just baked muffins. You aren't hungry, but you know she will be disappointed if you say no thanks. So you choose to say yes. You are still being honest with yourself and are well aware of why you said yes.

At a slightly more abstract level, it corresponds to having the ambition to be a clear person who knows what you will and will not do, and one who is able to stand firm when you need to and practice this in your daily life.

Be aware of why you choose to act as you do in specific situations. It may be that, in a certain conversation, you don't want to share your innermost thoughts with someone you don't trust, and that is quite okay. On the other hand, it is very easy to get into a pattern where you create too much drama and constantly say or promise things that are against what you really want. If you don't have the time and desire to go out and drink coffee, don't say yes just because you feel obligated.

Many of us have a tendency to accept an invitation if it falls at a time when we have a blank page in the calendar. But it's an honest thing to say no in that situation, that the rest of your week is overbooked and you need a quiet evening at home. Don't see it as a rejection of the person issuing the invitation. Stay on your own side of the road.

Too often we feel that we need an excuse because we are operating under the notion that it is wrong to say no. The result is that you can very easily get into a habit of dutifully and routinely saying yes to everything and completely forgetting to prioritize your own needs and be honest. Realize that for many others, your honesty can be an inspiration and a relief, and that they will, in turn, know that it is okay for them to say no when they need to.

On this very topic, the book *The Dance* made a big difference for me. Instead of just jumping up to say yes every time someone has a good idea, I am now inspired to pause first. The book takes dance as a metaphor for life. Author Oriah Mountain Dreamer writes, "Dance to the rhythms of your true self." Find your own way to move; dance to your own tune, rather than to the rhythms of others. Live your life according to your own values and who you are as a person.

Within that philosophy is also the message that it is important to realize that you are not perfect, that there are days when you don't feel 100 percent. It's okay. Accept it, because it's the only way you can "dance" authentically. Instead of trying to build a brand-new, perfect, and completely unrealistic sense of self, the author teaches you to focus on and accept the person you actually are— you are good enough as you are.

Remind yourself of this again and again. You are the master of the thoughts you think about yourself every day. Why not think of yourself as unique, fantastic, and beautifully imperfect? That is, after all, what you are.

LET GO OF AGE ANXIETY

Our age and our anxiety about the actual number on the birth certificate is a very concrete example of not facing the reality of our lives. If we do not accept our age, which is a matter of fact, we have a long way to go toward authenticity. Your relationship to your age is important to clarify, and if you prefer to keep how old you are a dirty little secret, it is important to find the answer why.

If I am comfortable with who I am, am able to accept both the good and the bad about myself, and am realistic and honest, then age cannot be a big issue. What is important is that I continue to develop and take good care of both my physical and mental health.

In some industries, it is difficult to land the big job after fifty, but in most companies, age in itself is no obstacle, especially in higher positions where experience is required to fill the role. A truly diverse, successful organization sees the value of having different generations working together and learning from each other.

IKEA is a "young" company, but for me it's not so much about age as it is about having a young mind-set. Generally, you aren't finished if you are fifty or sixty. In my view, it is entirely about the individual's motivation, ability to stay flexible, and willingness to learn new things, give back, mentor, and deliver results. Don't see yourself as a dinosaur. Continue to focus on opportunities and the future instead of feeling sorry for yourself and feeling that you are no longer worth anything. It is self-destructive.

As of this writing, I will soon turn fifty-five. I state my age with great pleasure. It's fantastic getting older. I have so much experience, so much to give, and so many new opportunities and challenges ahead of me. It is a matter of how we see ourselves, and changing the way you see yourself is always possible. Be open to new things and keep in touch with different generations.

Try mentoring, for example. The future is bright for women (and men) over fifty.

AUTHENTIC LEADERSHIP

I became aware of the importance of being authentic as I developed as a leader. Books along the way have helped me learn and create clarity for myself. They also exemplified where I was on my journey.

When I had my first management job at the Door Store, I was truly just surviving and my best friend was *The One Minute Manager* by Ken Blanchard. In my next management role at Stor, I learned the actual skills and responsibilities of being a good manager and I was holding on to Stephen Covey's *The 7 Habits of Highly Effective People*.

As IKEA store manager in Pittsburgh, I realized the kind of impact I had on people and how my behavior affected them, their performance, and the performance of the overall business. At this time, *On Becoming a Leader* by Warren Bennis shifted my understanding of the difference between leadership and management, and I came to understand that leadership starts with who I am as a person.

As HR manager for IKEA North America, I was faced with one of the most critical and stressful times of my leadership career. Between travel, family, and doing way too much, I had lost myself trying to do it all at a hundred miles per hour, firing on all cylinders. I discovered Oriah Mountain Dreamer's *The Dance*, which, as I have mentioned earlier, is an inspiring poem about dancing to the rhythms of your true self. Her message created a paradigm shift from dancing to other people's rhythms to finding and dancing to my own.

The Four Agreements by don Miguel Ruiz helped me get my head around what being yourself is really about.

As CEO of IKEA North America, *The Art of Possibility* by Rosamund Stone Zander and Benjamin Zander was such an inspiration and helped me discover that I am driven by possibilities. This is a book I handed over with huge importance to everyone joining our team, and I always handed it over by reading a quote in it from Marianne Williamson's *A Return to Love*, which still inspires me every day:

> Our deepest fear is not that we are inadequate. Our deepest fear is that we are powerful beyond measure. It is our light, not our darkness, that most frightens us. We ask ourselves, Who am I to be brilliant, gorgeous, talented, fabulous? Actually, who are you not to be? You are a child of God. Your playing small does not serve the world. There is nothing enlightened about shrinking so that other people won't feel insecure around you. We are all meant to shine, as children we do. We were born to make manifest the glory of God that is within us. It's not just in some of us; it's in everyone. And as we let our own light shine, we unconsciously give other people permission to do the same.

The people I worked with and who worked for me wanted to see me as a human being: a person who is vulnerable, who dares to stand up, and who recognizes that there are things I do not know or am not happy with. They need to feel secure that I will tell them when there are problems. As a leader, I like to be as honest and as clear as possible. Occasionally there are, of course, things you need to hold back because the timing is not always right. But if it concerns something that the employees ought to know, telling the truth and communicating is always the best policy.

I have always been Pernille and have been able to talk to people from all walks and positions in life. I never changed because of a new title. I also know that some people saw me differently because they could not separate me from the title. That's a reality I had to accept.

In Amsterdam, I wore the same clothes to the corporate office as I wore going out with friends in Chicago. I have sat and cried on a plane with a colleague who shared a very personal story, and when I go to our local sports bar to cheer on the family's favorite football team, the Pittsburgh Steelers, I'm the same person who attends the Women's Leadership Board at Harvard. People I have worked with know that I am me regardless of where we meet.

There are certainly many who have thought that I am a little crazy, being inspired and learning from poems and giving them to my management team. My greatest wish is that people around me find out who they are and discover their potential, their possibilities, and their personal strength, so I give away the very books that illuminated my own journey. Of course, I have read lots of traditional books on management, but they are not the kind of books that have defined and inspired me as a leader. They can be good to learn from, especially if you are new to being a leader, but they don't have the answers to everything when it concerns you in your very own role as leader.

I've always had my own personal, nontraditional management style. I lead based on my values, which are very personal. I am proud that, as a woman, I have been recognized. Even more importantly, I am grateful to be recognized for who I am.

TOOL

THE SIX LEVELS TO AUTHENTIC COMMUNICATION

I n my wallet, I have a laminated piece of paper describing the different levels we communicate with each other on—the different levels of authenticity. It is wisdom worth learning by heart.

Consider all the below scenarios in terms of walking along on the street and seeing a person you know.

Level 1

Avoidance: You choose to avoid and walk on without saying hello.

Level 2

Ritual: You choose the ritual of saying hello without stopping to talk.

Level 3

Passing Time: You stop and have a chat about how things are going, ask about family, work, etc., and wish the other person a good day.

Level 4

Playing Games: You speak with the person and you say, "You look great," even though you don't entirely mean it, or you say, "Good to see you. Let's get together and have a drink." This is basically when you say that you will call even though you don't really intend to do it.

Level 5

Collaboration: You ask each other with sincere enthusiasm and interest how things are going, and you arrange to meet next week to talk more. Or you honestly say that you are too busy at the moment, but that you would like to get together in about a month. You agree to get in touch and then make sure that you have each other's current contact information.

Level 6

Intimate Authenticity: The person can see that you aren't doing well. She is honest in telling you that you don't look like yourself and asks if everything is okay. You have been stressed or sick in the last few months and say that you have been having a hard time and haven't really felt like seeing anyone. She asks if there is anything she can do. You answer that you still don't have much interest in doing much of anything and don't have need for help at the moment. She thanks you for your honesty and says she would like to call you in a week to hear how you are doing if that is okay. You are happy and say yes. She calls as promised and you meet. You spend some time together and talk things out, and she listens patiently. Her support and sincerity boost you and your relationship.

Conclusion

Living authentically means being conscious of these six levels of communication. Which level do you use in which situation and in relation to whom? And are you conscious of your reasons? Being well versed in the six levels is also an effective practice when it comes to communicating in the workplace. As a leader, my ambition was to reach level five or six with my management team, but I didn't always succeed. Many communicate at level four or five.

Source: developed by Ulf Caap—inspired by Eric Berne and the book *Games People Play*.

Part 3

EMBRACING AND

CELEBRATING IMPERFECTION

"What if the question is not why am I so infrequently the person I really want to be, but why do I so infrequently want to be the person I really am?"

—Oriah Mountain Dreamer, *The Dance*

8

FACING THE CHALLENGES

The moment I became head of Ikea North America, everything changed. I still felt exactly like the same Pernille I had always been, but anyone who has been or is a leader knows exactly what I'm talking about. When you go from being a colleague to becoming the boss, a lot of challenges and resistance come with the added influence, the title, and the new, exciting tasks. That is just how it is sometimes. I had to accept it.

It was one of the hardest realities for me to face. I always encouraged people to be 100 percent honest with me and just continue to see me as Pernille, but not everyone could. I was the person in charge. I had the responsibility, and everyone looked at me as a manager, the top person. It is the very kind of responsibility that inherently can't be delegated to others.

In terms of relationships with colleagues, the dynamics changed with almost everyone. Even some of my closest friends suddenly saw me in a new way. They found it hard to relate to me easily, because no matter how much I tried to be the same as I always was, I was now the Boss. I lost some friends, and there were people who thought I should have treated them special. I lost contact with colleagues and one of my longtime friends, who was battling an incurable cancer. Thankfully, we have connected again, but she has said that she felt unable to talk to me over the years because she just couldn't get beyond my big, new title.

It was a tough pill to swallow, especially as relationships and the people in the organization are very important to me, and I made it a priority to be myself and be honest. I do not have a hidden agenda and am not absorbed in political games. People mean a lot to me, and I do not abandon my friends. Suddenly finding myself in a role where there were a lot of unwritten rules was a great personal challenge.

When I look back, I could have used my power as a manager, CEO, and president much more than I did. I could have played a more tactical game, and I could have used my position to say, "I don't care, because I'm the boss."

But I don't regret that for a minute; I am happy I didn't compromise who I am.

The big reward that came from having the top job was the privilege of having a lot of great people around me. I learned a lot about myself, and I developed an incredible resilience and ability to handle the ambiguity that comes with such a job.

The job was incredibly exciting and rewarding in many ways, and I don't consider the difficult moments and adjusting expectations about my relationships as a defeat. They were more like inevitable lessons that all leaders, at one point or another, have to learn.

STAY STRONG IN TIMES OF CRISIS

Being president of IKEA North America was my biggest career leap, and it coincided with a period when significant events were happening around me.

My first meeting in Sweden after taking the job happened just as the planes crashed into the World Trade Center on September 11, 2001. Shortly thereafter, the SARS epidemic broke out in Canada and a crazy sniper created panic in Washington, DC, and up and down the East Coast. People were paranoid, and suddenly there was a new climate in North America, a new culture to be a leader in.

Those kinds of unforeseen things happen, and even if they did not impact me directly, they affected the reality that I had to act in. Subsequently, there was an economic crisis and I was at the helm of a huge expansion: opening twenty-six new stores in eight years. Criticism was part of the job. Regardless of what you do, there will always be someone who is not satisfied. For me it became important to listen to what the negative voices had to say, but to truly hear what the people I could trust were saying.

I realized I was very good at communicating our vision and plan, and getting the organization behind it, so we could focus on the goals and tasks at hand. With such a significant growth plan, I had to prioritize with confidence and without wavering.

It meant, among other things, that my management team and I spent less time and effort on the daily operations of the existing stores than we normally would have. It's always a delicate balance, because the existing business must finance the expansion. It was hard for many to understand why we weren't focusing more on turnover, when the country's economy was spiraling downward along with sales in the stores.

It took a couple years to get our expansion and organization up and running well enough to be able to open so many new stores. An additional challenge at the time was that we were working with setting ourselves up to operate more simply and effectively. That meant fewer people would be in administration in the US head office, and instead, we would be strengthening the organization closest to the customers: the stores. The goal was to reduce 50 percent of the corporate staff and move them to the stores.

Each task was in and of itself a major effort, requiring a clear communication strategy. It was important to keep our eye on our objectives and not change direction. Of course, this agenda and these big changes created lots of questions from our staff. I realized it was my job to address these questions, and in this capacity, I didn't expect much help from the global headquarters on the other side of the world. I was it.

ASK FOR HELP

I knew I was responsible and took that part seriously—I would say too seriously and failed in asking for the help I truly needed. Support didn't come automatically from Europe or any other part of the world. In retrospect, I can see that I made the job a lot more difficult for myself and others. Based on my experience (yes, my mistakes), I recently said to a newly appointed executive who was overwhelmed by all that was new on her plate, "You can't be afraid to ask for help or good advice, and you have to ask for it early on."

Another example is a colleague who was totally disillusioned and overwhelmed by what life felt like at the executive level, and she had been alone with her thoughts for a while. When she was entrusted to that higher position, she did not want to show weakness and uncertainty. The result was that her frustration and disappointment piled up so high that she wanted to quit the job.

I imagine you have examples from your own life, so take this example as a reminder of how very important it is *at the beginning of a new challenge* to remember that sometimes you just don't know what you need to know, and you need to ask questions and ask for support. It has nothing to do with your qualifications or ability to do the job. If you do not speak up early, it can get harder to do so down the road. If too much time goes by, you might enter the zone of denial, and there, help is almost impossible to ask for because you don't want anybody to know you don't know.

Fortunately, I ended up going to my boss, a person whom I trusted tremendously and whom I had an extremely good working relationship with. Anytime I made a mistake, I was in doubt about how to move forward, or my confidence started to slide, I would talk to him and let him know how I felt. Sometimes I even asked him if he would rather have someone else do the job. His support proved to be massive, and he stressed again and again: "You are doing it right. Just keep going in the direction we've decided."

It strengthened me and gave me the confidence to continue on. Leadership challenges I had to handle myself. As a team player, it was hard to learn that even if you are trying to be honest and open, and have inspiring communication, you can't always get everyone on board. I can easily make my own decisions when necessary, but I'd rather take them on with my team. My experience is that the best decisions are made when everyone is heard, and together the team moves forward with a clear conclusion. As a leader, I believe that different minds and different thinking make for better decisions.

DON'T TAKE IT PERSONALLY

In my first year in the job, I could sense that not everyone had confidence in me, and some ignored what I said. Others did not trust me simply because I was a woman. Of course, I was offended and took it personally. I've always been happiest knowing everyone liked me, so I was in conflict. I was consumed with making a difference but could not please everyone. And when one is put together the way I am, it is never a good experience to have people against you. But I have learned to live with it, both through experience and through coaching by my closest colleagues and my husband.

You have to learn to separate yourself from the business, regardless of the work you do. When you stick your nose out and get in front of the crowd, you will most likely meet resistance. There is always the risk that someone will not agree with your message and your way of doing things. It has nothing to do with you and whether they like you or not. They are simply disagreeing with what you are doing. Over time, I have learned that you are never going to accomplish something if you try to make everyone happy and take things personally.

While I was trying to come to grips with this, I was also faced with the challenges from impatient employees and business partners who wanted immediate results and quick decisions from me as the leader. *Why doesn't she do something about this?* they all seemed to be thinking.

If you are constantly preoccupied with short-term problems and solutions, you'll never take the big step forward, because you will be overwhelmed by the many and constant small steps and expectations of others. You have to stay focused and consistent, and sometimes you have to live with the fact that great changes and achievements may only really become apparent when you've moved on to another job.

One of my big takeaways from that period was that it is not always enough to have good ideas. You need to prioritize your ideas, test them out on experts, get qualified input, test them out in real life, and be prepared to change your mind. Not all good ideas need to be implemented at once. Even good ideas require timing if you want others to be a part.

If you really want to change something, it takes time and strong commitment. You must be prepared to stay the course. As a leader, you also need to make sure your wishes and drive are aligned with the goals and focus of the company.

When I was most eager to implement a lot of ideas immediately rather than wait and see, I always had to remind myself that I was working for a company. My idea couldn't have any legs if it wasn't also an idea important for IKEA.

I especially needed to find this particular balance in my work to implement diversity in the organization. I had many ideas about how we could develop better business, broaden our customer base, develop the company culture, and be a better place to work by unleashing the potential of ethnic minorities and women. But from a company perspective, there was not the same urgency, and I had to adjust.

I have learned that just because I think something is a good idea, it does not necessarily mean that the rest of the organization will prioritize it. For example, I have always seen good business opportunities for IKEA selling their products and design expertise in a targeted manner to smaller firms, e.g., offices, retail shops, boutique hotels, cafés, and restaurants. We tried a little halfheartedly for a few years, but nothing came of it. Then, years later, it appeared on the agenda as a priority for all of IKEA, but still never with full steam and a clear plan.

All ideas need time to mature and develop, and we need to know when to push and when to lay off. The latter does not mean that we need to abandon the idea, but in a big company like IKEA, I learned to be patient and street smart.

Although I have a passion for change and the spirit to create it, I have also been humbled by how long it takes to create fundamental and true change. The time required for lasting change was something that I underestimated early on.

IBM's former chief diversity officer Ted Child made a big impression on me, and I remember his great advice at a diversity conference in the late nineties, that working with diversity is like taking the elevator: "You will have to stop on each floor." I have the same experience with women and ethnic minorities in IKEA's management group. If you drive too fast or take the elevator straight to the top floor, it may end up hurting more than it helps. It is simply too overwhelming. So when I wanted to lay the groundwork for my staff's success, it was important to realize that every individual needs time and experience—a solid foundation to build on. When they have the basics, they are ready to take bigger jumps and more responsibility—and to do so at a faster pace.

THE ART OF BUILDING A TEAM

You can do anything with the right team around you. It is a top priority for any good leader to surround themselves with the right people. When I first took on my job as president for IKEA in North America, I didn't have a dream team. It takes time to gather the right people. Even when I first accepted the job, it was quite clear that in addition to the task of expanding and changing the organization, I also had to make changes to the management team. I offered some of the existing managers positions outside the executive team, and the team had to function almost a year with several important positions open. At the same time, I had to keep one of the managers who did not support me, but I absolutely needed his knowledge and experience, which no one else had at the time. In hindsight, I could have prioritized addressing this and finding his replacement much earlier, but with other openings, I let it go for a while.

Note to self: don't say yes to doing so many things at one time, and always prioritize putting the right team in place.

Having to fire people is an unavoidable task as a manager. My starting point is always to make sure there has been clear communication about expectations, and give people a chance to make things right. If the employee does not live up to responsibilities, doesn't make the necessary improvements, and doesn't take warnings seriously, there is no way around it. When it comes down to it, I can fire people, but it should never be easy, and a professional process is critical. My first experience in firing employees was when I worked in Miami. Back then, I was inexperienced. I did it very unprofessionally, and the company didn't have a good process in place.

If I am clear and honest in my communications and explain things properly, most people understand. A pink slip rarely comes out of the blue and is usually the end result of a number of conversations with the employee, which has taken place over a certain period of time. I believe that firing someone is a failure of both the manager and the employee. Most people want to succeed, and as leaders we have a big responsibility to coach our staff to perform and develop, and employees have to take responsibility for their own performance and development. Neglecting to address a performance issue with an employee is very common, as it often seems like it'd be easier to ignore it and hope it will go away. Long term, it will have some truly negative consequences for the morale of the organization, and it doesn't serve the underperforming employee either.

There may be some cases when you are not the one making the decision about letting an employee go, but as the boss, you have to handle it. In such situations, you have a message that you have been assigned to deliver, and it does not help to try to sugarcoat it. The recipient's reaction is their responsibility; you can't control it. Most organizations have a clearly defined procedure for laying people off, and it is important that you always take responsibility for your employees, both when it goes well and when it goes bad.

Even if you don't mix emotion into it, letting someone go is never easy. If you start to feel comfortable with this aspect of your job, something is wrong. It should affect you, and you can always do your part to make the situation less painful by being human, open, and honest.

OPEN COMMUNICATION

My experience with having straightforward conversations came in very handy when we had to restructure the North America corporate office. The goal was not to part with a lot of employees, but there were still one hundred and fifty who needed to be moved to other positions and jobs outside the office.

Over the years, we had built up a large and bureaucratic organization, and it was my responsibility to make it more simple and effective. It was overwhelming and seemed contradictory to have a large reduction of people at the same time we were facing a significant expansion period. At the same time, it was a great opportunity to use the best resources in the stores and set the right organization for the future.

We involved the employees in the process and focused communication on the overarching goals: to give the stores more local responsibility, strengthen the competence in the stores, and be closer to the customers.

We didn't talk about layoffs because it was a last resort in case an employee did not want to move to another location or new job function, or if the solutions we proposed just couldn't work.

Employees want to know that you are honest and caring while giving direction and bringing vision to the company. With the exception of a few employees who were dissatisfied and didn't trust me, my experience was that the staff mostly had great loyalty to each other, to our organization, and to me. Even the people who criticized me or disagreed with me were also incredibly dedicated.

In 95 percent of the cases, I got the same open communication in return for what I put out. Many like to be a part of change and develop new ways of working but can't see how. Therefore, they need to have a clear message, be met with confidence, and feel involved.

As a leader, it's easy to say, "We need to develop better work processes, be innovative, and start lots of new initiatives," but not everyone is interested in taking chances and going off on new adventures. I have learned that I can't automatically expect that everyone else is as interested in renewal as much as I am—or is as willing to follow the basic recipe of "this is a good idea; let's do it."

It's generally accepted in business that only about 10 percent of most business strategies get implemented. Execution of our ambitions is the biggest challenge of all. It's a lot easier to point out and describe the what than it is to get it done.

My experience tells me that we must listen to everyone around the table. Getting others' opinions can lead to better decisions and a better end result. In a group, there will be someone who says that the idea is not thought through well enough, that the projected outcome is not based on enough facts, or that the implementation is impossible due to lack of necessary competence. Not everyone will jump on board with the idea. In the moment, it can feel like resistance, like a table of devil's advocates, but it is a natural part of effective decision making.

Though it is irritating to have a good idea slowed down, it is invaluable to have critical feedback. We all have different strengths and ways of thinking. One of the most important tasks as a leader is to build a diverse team of people around you with different backgrounds, skills, and learning styles to complement you. Do not be afraid of their strengths, and be open to what they bring.

The job of creating a good leadership team is never done. It takes serious attention to find talent, develop the team members, and support them as they grow. It's about deciding which competencies are needed for the future and how you can go about developing them. Succession planning, having diverse people in the pipeline with the necessary skills, is critical. It takes time. For many years, I had fantastic people around me (not perfect, of course, but fantastic). They were on board, worked relentlessly toward our goals, and complemented and developed me. Together, we achieved great results.

GROWTH FROM ADVERSITY

When I talk about obstacles and adversity, it is important for me to emphasize how necessary they are for growth. You develop the most when you are confronted with something new and difficult.

The challenge of the reorganization gave me great strength, and I learned to find strength even in the toughest of times.

During my career, I have not faced big personal failures, but I have experienced resistance and many smaller failures. There have been situations that I've thought were big and overwhelming, but I had to find a way to handle them. I have discovered myself as a resource, and I have trusted and believed that I could handle it—often I jumped back to my acting experience in seventh grade.

My biggest problem in terms of resistance has actually been that I always try to be positive, mediate, and get the best out of a situation. While in many ways it is a strength, the reverse is also true: sometimes I have not faced reality or have been slow to accept it.

To accept that things are going poorly is one of the hardest things for me. I naturally see the glass half-full. It takes me longer to face reality than it does for others, especially when it's my own idea or an idea that I have been behind 100 percent. I have a hard time letting go of the feeling that a solution is there to be found.

It is a very fine balance to be driven toward a decided goal and to stop and be realistic. I have been involved in projects that came close to being closed down but eventually came to fruition, and others that lost energy and, for several reasons, made no sense to continue.

On the other hand, I do not find it difficult to say sorry when I first recognize that maybe it was not the best idea. I apologize in many circumstances—with my husband and my children as well as at work. My family can attest to my stubbornness, but when I find out that it was me who was wrong, I am not afraid to admit that I made a mistake and am not perfect. Saying sorry is quite powerful. It changes the situation completely, and gives people the chance to see you in another way. All of a sudden, there's not as much to discuss. If I say I am sorry, then it is up to the other party to accept the apology or not.

CRUSHED DREAMS OF HOLLYWOOD

When I first moved to the United States, I remember saying several times, "It's not so bad," even though things obviously were bad. If I knew then what I know today, it probably wouldn't have taken me two years to realize that our design company was not going to be a success and that the problems my business partner and I had could not be solved by just working harder.

I was certainly driven by my refusal to give up. I was so focused on reaching my goal that I forgot to stop and see what was going on around me.

The same thing happened when I moved to Los Angeles in 1987. My dream of driving across the United States—to Los Angeles, to Hollywood—came true. To begin with, I stayed with a good friend of my family. Quite quickly I got an apartment in the same building, but Los Feliz wasn't the Hollywood most of us would have thought of at the time. It wasn't especially safe walking on the streets at night, and there certainly were no Hollywood stars nearby. But I started my job at Stor glad to be in Los Angeles, although it wasn't quite what I had dreamed of.

After the honeymoon came reality, in the form of quite a few unfortunate and frustrating events. First, a massive earthquake hit the city. I was driving when it happened, and suddenly the radio went out and it felt like I had four flat tires. I totally freaked out. One of the many aftershocks came when I was sitting with my friend in her apartment. Suddenly, I felt very far away from home.

A few weeks later, I was driving on the freeway about to change lanes and didn't notice that the car in front of me had come to a halt. The taillights were out and I drove straight into it. Luckily nothing happened to me or the other driver, but the experience shook me. My already-squeezed budget certainly wasn't geared for repairs and rising insurance premiums.

One night, I woke up to discover my whole room brightly illuminated and the window hot. The big high-rise being built opposite my apartment building was going up in flames. With plenty of dry palm trees in the yard, there was great risk that the fire would quickly spread. We were evacuated, and the only thing I could manage to take with me was my car. Fortunately, a strong wind blew in, taking the flames in the other direction and allowing firefighters to get the fire under control.

Job-wise, my first days in Hollywood were anything but relaxing, to say the least. Stor was a new company with ambitions of having Ikea-like success from day one. The customer base and sales never lived up to the high expectations, and maybe that was why I experienced enormous pressure on all fronts from the beginning. Whatever I did and suggested wasn't good enough. I felt inexperienced and incompetent, and my confidence took more than one blow. I had come from the experience of being in small retail stores and was now in big business. Before I had managed only a few direct reports, and all of a sudden I was supervising fifty, including a department head who directly undermined me for the first several months because he thought he was better qualified for the job than I was.

To sum up everything about obstacles: You need to prepare yourself for the fact that it will not necessarily be easy to reach your goals, whether it's an exciting job, a high position, a marriage, or another dream you want to reach. In the beginning, maybe you will have lots of support, but it is almost impossible to avoid all resistance. Then again, if you give up, you won't get far.

Therefore, it is dangerous to believe that all development and all roads are a straight line from A to B. It is enough to know that you want to get to B, but the road will likely be a tortuous route. There will be times when you hang upside down, completely confused, and can't see how you'll ever get through. But accept it. It's part of the process—it's part of life. Even if you have to fall into a deep hole as I did.

As for Hollywood, I quickly moved from there to the more peaceful and quiet Orange County, where I lived for two years and met my wonderful husband.

TOOL

TAKING ON A NEW CHALLENGE

Taking on a new job responsibility or a new management position is often an opportunity to start fresh and create a new platform for yourself. It is really important to consider this before just rushing in and bringing all the old with you automatically. Here are some things to consider to get you started on the right foot.

1. Make sure that your values are aligned with your company's values before you start.
2. Find out what the company expects from you. Ask for clarity during the job interview. Make sure this is really what you want and that it will move you in the right direction—both short- and long-term.
3. Arrive new and enthusiastic, but don't be surprised or feel defeated if you are met with hesitation or skepticism. It is human and natural to be leery of someone new.
4. Be humble. Do not come roaring in like a one-person show with all the answers. Take time to understand the business, the company culture, and the different ways of working.
5. Show trust and recognize your colleagues' skills and experience—you can learn from them.
6. Talk and listen to employees and colleagues. Hear what they expect, what they believe they can offer, and how they see you can make improvements together. Many times they have the answers. They have been living with the problems.

7. Change is not nearly as overwhelming and difficult if you get the team and the people around you involved in the process.
8. Be patient and take your time. If you try too hard, jump to conclusions quickly, and act too impulsively, you run the risk of making the wrong decision and it can be difficult to undo it and change later, after you know what you are doing and have more input.
9. Be honest and open in your communication.
10. Do not sit behind a closed office door ordering changes to employees you aren't in touch with. Manage while walking around, talking to people, connecting, and keeping your ears open. It can help you in your everyday decision making. I personally have always preferred an open office space, where we sit together, not separated by a row of private offices.
11. Remember that many people have been committed to your predecessor and you don't automatically win over their trust. There will always be some who don't support you. Don't focus too much on them, but be humble and open to other points of view.
12. Learn to differentiate between personal criticism and professional disagreement.
13. Apply a lot of energy to putting the right team around you. Focus on different competencies, as well as diversity skills, leadership styles, and experiences. Separate yourself from those who go behind your back and decide to work against you. Rely on competent and capable people who will support, challenge, and complement you.
14. Don't be afraid of asking for help and advice from the top, and do it early on, when you are new and naturally don t know. Find a mentor. If you wait too long, it can be embarrassing to ask for help.

15. Take responsibility for your own introduction to the company, and have a plan for what you need in order to be successful. Take full ownership for your own performance and leadership development. It's your life.

ACCEPT ADVERSITY

As you take on challenges in your life, the question is not whether you will face adversity, but how to handle it when it appears.

1. Drop the illusion that you can reach your goal without bumps in the road. Prepare your mind.
2. Along the way, the quicker you accept things as they actually are, the quicker you can decide what to do and move on. Let go of any denial. The sooner you accept difficulty or a defeat, the sooner you can live through your feelings and move on. No one likes to have a bucket of cold water dumped on her head. It's okay to be sad and make room for all emotions, but don't get stuck here.
3. Write down the specific issue and try to get to the essence of the problem, the core. Take some time to distance yourself from the problem; don't take it personally and do not give up.
4. Once you have accepted the reality as it is, ask yourself: What now? What can I learn from this situation? What is the best step forward? Do not forget to include and call upon your nearest and dearest in the process.
5. Any major change requires hard work. Recognize that struggles, setbacks, and problems are an inevitable and indispensable part of the process. Setbacks can give us the best experience and learning, as they force us to take a few steps back and are key to moving forward with new vigor and energy.

6. Console yourself with the fact that even some of the world's most successful people have had setbacks along the way. People like Nelson Mandela, Steve Jobs, Hillary Clinton, Sonia Sotomayor, and President Barak Obama all met adversity along their journey but never gave up.

9

LETTING GO OF ILLUSIONS
AND FACING REALITY

Fast-forwarding a few cities, jobs, and roughly ten years later to when I started my stint as HR manager for IKEA North America: I was in Philadelphia facilitating a two-day diversity strategy meeting with senior managers. In the morning, my arm was numb. It felt like it was asleep. Over the course of the day, it got worse and worse. As I was driving back to the hotel that afternoon with my colleague, I told him I had this strange feeling in my arm and joked that maybe I was having a stroke.

He replied quite seriously, "I hope you know that I do not think that is funny at all." The longer I drove, the more I sensed things getting worse. I was about to black out. I had no idea what was happening to me. I no longer had control and was afraid that I would lose control of the car. We were driving on the highway, and I remember clearly debating with myself if I should get off the next exit or continue. I realized how crazy that was and I told my colleague, "We are getting off the highway. I don't feel good," and he dialed 911.

They asked us to drive to a parking lot nearby, where they would come within a few minutes. It wasn't long before I was lying in the back of an ambulance. The very calming female paramedic said, "You're not having a heart attack—just relax."

That it even occurred to me to consider driving down the highway says everything about where I was in my life. That was why I had come so far in my career: I always just continued. But luckily, that day, I took the exit.

The paramedics drove at full speed, sirens on and lights flashing, and my friend followed behind in the car. Even though he had been told that he couldn't run red lights as well, he did anyway. Tears rolled down my cheeks the whole way. I could only see my feet and the red lights, and I remember thinking, *So this is success? Here I am away from my home, my family, my children, and my life. This can't really be success . . .*

In the hospital, I was immediately put into capable hands, and it was quickly confirmed that there was nothing physically wrong. My friend and I both cried.

"It will be the best gift you've ever had," my friend said. The only thing I thought was: *What in the world is he talking about?* The doctor said that my panic attack had been triggered by stress that had built up over a long time. He recommended going to my doctor, for medicine but also to address what changes I needed to make. But I never did. My friend and I jumped back in the car, right back on the very same road, and went to dinner to digest what had just happened. At the time, I was mostly embarrassed and, am sure, deep inside, afraid the world would see I was actually human. At dinner, I called my husband and told him I had had a small issue, but I was okay. I didn't want to alarm him.

Today I can see that my panic attack had been a long time coming, because everything had piled up and because, like it is for many others, it was easier to continue than to look reality directly in the face.

At that time, leading up to the anxiety attack, I had been married for ten years, my kids were six and eight years old, and I had come far in my career. In order to keep everything together, I had stretched myself by living in Pittsburgh and commuting to Philadelphia, where my job was at IKEA headquarters. In this way, my husband could continue his career, we could continue to stay in Pittsburgh as a family, and I could continue to develop my career and do what I loved. I had a very flexible setup and didn't have to go every week at a certain time. My boss had said that his minimum requirement was attending his meetings.

For many months leading up to the anxiety attack, there was a lot of traveling and even more months where I tried to pretend that I had made the right decision. At work, I didn't want people to see that I was not perfect. The same was true at home. When we had friends over on weekends, after I had come home from a trip, I was always on. It was important to keep going, to be positive and keep it all together. When I came home, I wanted to be with my husband and kids, and we all wanted to see our friends. I felt a tremendous responsibility, and if things didn't work, it was—according to my logic—my fault.

HIGH-SPEED DENIAL

After my anxiety attack, I talked a little with the colleague who had been with me, but at home I pretended it hadn't happened. I simply ignored the incident and continued on at full speed. As I write this, I can't believe my own reaction, my denial.

At that time, my husband and I were in one of the most difficult phases of our marriage, and in large ways, we lived two different lives. I traveled a lot, leaving my husband alone with the kids, and when I got home, I was tired, brought work with me, and focused on the kids but not on him. Life just went on like this, and it was easier and easier to ignore the problems.

My own experience has convinced me that it is very hard to warn others who are just about to hit the wall. When I ask other women, "Why are we so smart and so stupid at the same time?" I am speaking just as much about myself as I am about anyone else.

Once, I gave a presentation to a group of Italian businesswomen in Rome. I spoke among other things about what my anxiety attack had taught me. Afterward, a woman stood up and told of a similar situation and then posed the burning, relevant question: "Are we able to do something for these women who drive too fast and don't stop until they wreck and are forced to?"

My answer—then and now—is that we sadly have to feel and face reality on our own. When it is about doing many physical and practical tasks, we are incredibly smart, but once it comes to our own well-being, we are actually quite stupid. Many of us do things we would never dream of recommending others do.

When you are racing down the highway and receive well-meaning comments about driving too fast, you can't hear them—or you don't dare listen. I couldn't listen then. My colleague often said to me, "You don't listen to your body." He also always said that I'm good at helping everyone other than myself, which I think applies to many. As women, we have a responsibility to take care of ourselves. It's just very hard to help each other see this because we are often not receptive to good advice before it is too late, before we get an insight that changes things radically.

I hope at least that you hear stories like mine and, on that basis, begin to take some time for yourself. I hope you will try to assess your situation, so you make some adjustments and changes before you hit the wall. I came to the realization the hard way when I was in my forties. My wish for you is that you think about it before. Is it wise to run on all cylinders at home and at work, with no time to reflect on yourself? Remember that it's okay not running on all cylinders at all times. I learned to get help with some things. Often our pride is a greater obstacle than money when it comes to prioritizing—or getting help.

SHIFTING INTO LOWER GEAR

Since that day, I learned what I can physically do to feel better and am much more aware of what is going on with me. If I have traveled too much and am sitting on a plane, my heart beating fast, it is a sign that I just need to slow myself down and relax. I shouldn't turn on the computer and start reading emails. Instead, I should read something for fun, watch a movie, or just be still and focus on my breathing.

I also became better at not arranging too much, not filling my agenda. Previously, I would typically accept invitations out, even after a long day. Now I am clear on what works and when I need to rest.

It was a big change at the time to not check emails on the weekend and not be on the phone all the time. I could easily work twenty-four hours a day. I learned to set boundaries for myself—it's my responsibility. Work is indeed infinite, and there is always more we can do.

Even today, I drive down the highway with a little too much speed. I'm more conscious of it and can slow down to sixty-five, but I am never the person puttering along in the slow lane. I also learned to pause. For years, people had been joking that when in meetings with me, you would have to ask for breaks. It still happens but more seldom.

For many years, I tried to convince myself that I could easily accomplish more work and make more of everything, that it was merely a question of doing just a little extra. Seen from the outside, it is totally frantic. As my mentor says, "We can all handle the heavy workload for a limited period, but then it starts to break us down. It is necessary to balance your focus on work with a focus on you."

STRESS SAVED MY MARRIAGE

Without stress, I might have paid the price with my marriage. The subsequent work I did on myself made me aware of my inappropriate routines and the holes in my relationships. My husband and I have always loved and focused on our life together, but it has also been important for us to give each other room. We never wanted to stop each other from doing what the other loves as an individual.

The problem was that I just became more and more distracted. When I was home, I was tired and stressed, couldn't seem to focus, and was not really present. This impacted my husband especially. Yet I did everything to prevent my busy work and travel schedule from having consequences on the children. You may recognize the pattern.

When the children were small, I would talk with them on the phone every morning, and I can remember my son, at the age of five or six, said he was upset when I wasn't home. He was a little afraid to talk to me, as my husband didn't want them to make me sad when I was away. When I would come home, I would spend all the time I could with the kids. I had missed them and always had the best of intentions. I wanted to catch up and cram in as much as possible, but often found myself distracted and stressed out. When I look back, it was just a really tough period for both my husband and me. We did not have enough time and energy for each other—and at times, ourselves.

When I started to work more on my personal development, it gave us, as a couple, an opportunity to stop and look at what was happening. We were and still are each other's best friend and soul mate, but back then we had to face the fact that even the best relationship is fragile. Even a marriage based on a foundation of passion and friendship needs work and attention, and can go wrong if you don't nurture it.

We could have ended up divorced, and in a strange way, my anxiety attack saved our marriage because it forced me to stop and take a very close look at how I was living my life. It became a catalyst for both of us to reflect on our relationship.

Who was my behavior good for? It was good for IKEA. That is not to say that all I did was for the company's benefit. My private life was just a result of the way I had chosen to work. I was there for IKEA and my children, but not for my husband or myself. Quite unconsciously, I was operating on autopilot.

We spent almost a year talking through every aspect of our marriage and our relationship. Some months were very intense, with the big questions hanging in the air: Can we save it? Can we live the life we want? Sometimes I wasn't sure how it would end.

I had to be very honest with myself and face some unpleasant realities. How could I see myself as a good person who wanted the best for everyone and at the same time be so noncaring toward the ones closest to me—and even toward myself? All so I could just keep on going without stopping to reflect on what really mattered.

At the time, I was obviously not in touch with my inner strength or potential, or any of the other things I have mentioned. I had lost my footing, was not ready to talk to anyone, and refused to face reality. I had pushed myself into a corner and couldn't see the solution. It took me at least a year after the anxiety attack before I began to understand and accept what had hit me.

I said yes to participating in a personal development program in Sweden, and this became another turning point—my aha moment and the start of the journey to find my footing and grounding again. Without that week, I might still be in serious denial.

LET GO OF AN UNREALISTIC LIFE

During this personal development week, through different exercises, we discussed what was going on in our lives both personally and professionally, and I certainly realized I had to change a few things in my life.

I had lived under the illusion that I could handle it all. I had been living an unrealistic life, and I felt it personally, physically, and mentally. Afterward, it was so crystal clear to me how completely unrealistic it was that I had imagined my life would work under those circumstances.

I took huge responsibilities on in my job that weren't necessary. I took things too personally and let my job get too close to me. As HR manager, you see all the things that do not work, and even if you know what needs to be addressed, you don't have the formal power to make it happen. It truly felt like pushing an elephant up the stairs.

I put a lot of my energy behind diversity, leadership, part-time and domestic partnership benefits, and women in leadership, and I had this urge to make life easier and better for our employees. I have always had a tendency to take other people's problems to heart, wanting to make life easier for others—behavior that usually doesn't help anyone long-term and certainly not me.

The important thing is to become aware of your limitations. Surrender all illusions that you can manage everything. Somehow I lived under the illusion that it was my responsibility to fix everything. The facilitator of the program challenged me at some point during the week and asked why I always sat on the edge of my chair, leaning in, focusing on others, always ready to engage. "Why don't you just sit back?" she asked.

Her question made me very uncomfortable without quite knowing why. I could feel some of the things that I had been ignoring slowly rising to the surface. The whole purpose of a personal development program is to reflect on our personal lives—what we are happy about, what we need to address, what we need to change—and as the week moved on, I had a chance to take a good hard look at the whole thing.

It was emotional and tough to get out, but it was also an enormous relief. I had people around whom I had come to trust, and they were great coaches for me. It was an emotional week, but one of the milestones in my life. Today there are issues I am quite comfortable with and happy to share in this book. I learned, among other things, that I had lived my life on autopilot and lost a lot of my emotions. As I piled more and more on my plate, I got more and more disconnected from myself and my family. I was finally able to understand how that impacted my relationship with my husband. I, who had always wanted to give to others and considered myself a person with a big heart, suddenly could not feel my heart. I realized that you have to do something for yourself to be able to help others—just like when a flight attendant tells you to put on your own oxygen mask before helping the people who are sitting next to you.

EMBRACE IMPERFECTION

During the personal development week in Sweden, I realized that facing my shortcomings and stress wasn't so dangerous after all. I appreciated what a difference it had made for me, so a few years later, when I was president of IKEA North America, I felt it was time to pay it forward.

I started "I & IKEA" for sixteen top female managers in the United States. They were all very successful, but something was holding them back from taking new steps in their lives, personally as well as professionally. We met for three days at a time, every six to eight weeks over the course of a year.

I was in a group with four others, and one of the exercises was an especially eye-opening experience for me. We each received the same set of cards, each one indicating a specific aspect of life. Our task was to put them in the order that we prioritized them in our lives. The three other women placed the family card first, and when it was my turn, I could easily have done the same. Then it struck me that I couldn't. Because if my family truly came first, would I really be living my life the way I was?

My family is incredibly important to me, but I have had to face the fact that if I do not feel good about myself, I can't be there for my family. If I am not doing something meaningful, something I'm passionate about, where I contribute and make a difference, I am not fulfilled. If I am doing the things I love, I am a better me. Throughout my life, I have chosen to have an exciting and challenging job, but there are times when I have let the job completely take over and have lost myself. That is when everything has gone wrong on all fronts.

Not putting the family card first challenges a lot of the expectations and pressure we are laying on ourselves as mothers.

Since I didn't put the family card first, we had a really good discussion about the illusion we all have about being perfect mothers. We were all struggling with doing what we loved and at the same time living up to the traditional role of a "good" mother. Superwoman doesn't exist. It's simply about being realistic and realizing it's okay to not be perfect.

We each found ourselves in similar straitjackets: I must be a perfect mother, a perfect wife, the perfect employee, perfect friend; have a perfect home; look perfect; and the list goes on. Together, we abandoned the concept of a "perfect" mother and embraced the idea of "mothers of imperfection"; it was a new and liberating truth.

There is much guilt and bad conscience associated with being a mother. Even though I personally never had the ambition to be the perfect mother, I have struggled with the decision I made not to be a stay-at-home mother. Not because I felt I was wrong, but because there was a lot of pressure from the external world, and I put pressure on myself. My children have grown up with me working; I have prioritized them in my life and fortunately have been able to plan so I didn't miss important events for them, but I wasn't there every day, all the time. Did they want me to spend more time at home? Yes, that was sometimes true, but they also knew that I was not the one who sat on the floor playing with them or reading to them for hours. It's not my personality. They have grown up to become great human beings and they agree I am imperfect. They also cannot imagine me having been home all the time, and they swear they wouldn't have turned out as well if I had.

For me it has been harder to accept that I wasn't the perfect employee. When our I & IKEA group came to the insight that we were "imperfect mothers," it helped me break down the other illusions I had about being perfect. I'm good at something but not everything, and that is okay.

Allow yourself to face the problems, be realistic, and celebrate your imperfection. The moment you dare to see things as they are and recognize your weaknesses, you accept them, and they will take up less room. An imperfect mother is not a bad mother. She's just human. Using the word *imperfect* actually unleashes incredible strength and unbelievable power.

There we sat, four women who all lived stressed, unrealistic, and ambitious lives with a tendency to strive for perfection. It could just as well have been any number of other women or men. It was a great aha moment for all of us—a huge liberation. It led to great discussions and to the writing of our song, "Mothers of Imperfection."

It was a new headline for us.

THE DEVIL CREATED MULTITASKING

As soon as you recognize and accept imperfection, you will find the pressure goes down. The power of this awareness functions in and of itself as a valve: suddenly you can let some air out of the system. It brings peace…and room to be your honest self.

I remember how my own mother, who every night at eight sighed as she sat down to put up her feet, saying, "Oh, it feels good to sit down. I have been on my feet all day." How often have I heard myself say the same to my husband? His response has always been, "Now whose fault is that?"

You don't have to be a genius to figure out that if you are running around from seven in the morning to seven in the evening, doing a million things over the course of the day, it isn't a healthy way to live. We are a generation of women with a lot on our plates in comparison to our mothers. We would like to have good jobs; we would also like to keep ourselves in shape, have beautiful homes, and be good wives, mothers, and girlfriends, and there is absolutely nothing wrong with any of that. The problem is that we want it all at once, and we want it all to be perfect.

Women are equipped with web-like brains that have the ability to multitask. Science confirms that men and women's brains are different. Men's brains operate in a very focused way, while women's brains branch like the threads of a spider's web. We can easily sit in the middle of a discussion and be thinking of a hundred other things. When a man watches television, he typically isn't really thinking of anything else. In contrast, most women usually have one or more other trains of thought running while they are in the midst of doing any given thing. Of course, it can be a great advantage to be able to grasp several things at one time, but in the long run, it is probably a disadvantage.

This built-in feature makes us able to run for a long time before our bodies or souls says no. Today, women keep up with men in the workplace; we can run big organizations, but we haven't lowered our expectations at home. We want that to be perfect too. We just pile more and more on our plates without giving ourselves the opportunity to say no—or say yes, *but not now*.

Indeed, I believe that we have given ourselves an impossible task. We have to face the fact that we can't stand in front of a large buffet and taste everything at once. Accept that you need to take one thing at a time. Accept that maybe you are not the best at everything. Otherwise, you end up living a very unhealthy life emotionally.

When I finally faced my negative patterns and routines, it became important for me to focus on myself, my husband, and my children—and not just IKEA. My husband and I started spending more time together—a weekend alone, a good dinner, concerts— and scheduled it in the calendar. I became better at planning vacations and work, so I could have more time with my kids, and, for the first time since I was single, I got into an exercise routine and splurged on massages.

I was serious about living a different life—a life where I was present. The big change has really been being aware, present, setting limits and boundaries, and having the courage to say no.

The good news is that it worked. And continues to work. The potentially bad news is that it takes time. For me it wasn't a dramatic change from one day to the next. Instead, it has been constant development and exercise to listen to my body and connect with my gut. Or put in another way: it has been constant work ever since and always will be. But it's work that pays off.

THE BEST FAREWELL

Daring to face reality has probably been one of the most liberating experiences of my life. Although I came to the realization the hard way, I have to agree with the cliché that it can be a gift to hit the wall.

Let me give you another personal example of a situation where facing reality made a huge difference. My father was very ill with cancer in 2004. It is really hard when a person you have been close to all your life suddenly becomes seriously ill. The message was very clear from the beginning: nothing could be done. There was no hope or cure. The process of accepting that you can't do anything is a tough and emotional experience. For me, it quickly became clear that the sooner I accepted it, the more I would be able to make of the remaining time we would have together.

Today, I am very grateful for the time I had with my dad at the end of his life. Because I'm wired to find solutions, I very easily could have spent a lot of precious time trying to find doctors and seeking alternative methods and treatments around the world.

But accepting that death was close allowed me to let go of my fear. Most importantly, my father could feel that I was not afraid. In the last months of his life, we consequently discussed a lot of topics he was probably afraid to touch on with others. I was able to talk with him in a more open way, because I had accepted that he would soon die. It was the best way I could say good-bye to him.

This probably makes it sound much easier than it was, but no matter how hard, painful, sad, and scary it is to face reality, it is the only way forward. The quicker we get there, the better. Once we have accepted reality, we can start looking for life ahead.

My own downturn is a good example of what happens when we are unable to accept what is right in front of our noses. It took me more than a year to actually be able to see the reality and the reason behind my anxiety—and only then could I start on a new path.

TOOL

WHAT STRESS TAUGHT ME

Writing down what stress has taught you is a meaningful exercise. It is by reflecting on our experiences that we get insights about the future.

1. Don't lose yourself. Stress is a result of losing control over your life when something dramatic and unexpected happens (an accident, death, serious illness, etc.) or when we let others take control (like a boss, a spouse, or a job). The former is relatively obvious to identify and to get help in managing. The latter sneaks up on you over time; you don't see it, but it gets worse and worse. It can be hard to realize before it is too late and something dramatic happens, like my anxiety attack. Often people around us see what is happening; it's clear to them, but we deny it and aren't receptive to their worry or advice. I have learned to listen to myself and to the danger signs. If I wake up feeling nervous in my gut and apprehensive, I know better than to push it under the rug now. It is a sign for me to take a closer look. I also listen to people around me when someone says, "You are always so busy." I don't just ignore them anymore. I pay attention to whether I am back on my old track.

2. Awareness creates change. Tiger Woods was once asked what changes he expected to make now that he, as a black man, had become the highest ranked golfer in the world. He answered that he believes that awareness creates change. His statement has stayed with me. The awareness about my stress has been the biggest change driver for me.

3. Set your own boundaries. One of my colleagues once said that IKEA is addictive and the work is so exciting that you can easily get consumed. I know now that it is not IKEA's responsibility but my own to set the boundaries. Work can't be everything in your life and take all your time and energy. It is important to carve out room and live life outside of work with family, friends, and all your different interests. I have never seen myself as an exercise fanatic, but I have recognized that it is extremely important for me to engage in physical activity, whether it is working out at the gym, swimming, yoga, or simply taking a walk. Today I am more physically active and, if I am not, I don't feel good. It is a great way to take a break and get some distance from things. It helps bring me in balance.

10

FORGET ABOUT WORK-LIFE BALANCE

C reating the perfect work-life balance has often been hailed as the perfect solution to a busy work and family life. We have convinced ourselves that we can create a perfect balance between work and family life. In my experience, it has become another quest for perfection, which is pretty impossible to reach.

I believe we can forget about a work-life balance. We only have one life, and it's about prioritizing and making conscious choices all the time, every single day, so we can be at ease with ourselves and feel good.

The concept of work-life balance has come into our lives because today it is normal for both parents to work outside the home. Most families have two parents who work; for married couples alone the number is 50 percent, according to a 2013 report from the Bureau of Labor Statistics, US Department of Labor (Employment Characteristics of Families). For many families, it is not a choice, as both parents have to work for financial reasons; for others, it's for personal reasons, but the fact remains that it has increased the pressure on both men and women. If your child is sick, one of you must stay home. Every day is about sharing the responsibility of dropping kids off at school at a certain time and picking them up, and then there are the thousands of practical things that have to be taken care of as well. Fortunately, men have become much more involved in the family than they were just twenty-five years ago, but it is still so difficult for many families to make it all work.

Balance is an organic movement; it doesn't stay in one place all the time, and a good life requires conscious decisions and great awareness, and most importantly an acceptance of the imperfect balance. We can live with and deal with a lot of not-so-perfect scenarios if we agree on it and do not expect perfection. We need to be flexible but realistic in order to create internal balance.

We can't just add and add things to our life without stepping back and taking a look at the full picture, our complete life.

I can remember very clearly one situation when I was completely unrealistic and kept piling things on. It was when I was offered the job as HR manager for IKEA North America and asked my husband if he wanted to move to Philadelphia.

"Are you out of your mind? How can you ask if I think it is a good idea to move to Philadelphia? We are just starting to feel settled here in Pittsburgh."

This was a pretty understandable response. He has always accepted that I have earned more and had a higher position than him. He has always known his mission in life, and he loved his job at the time as a middle school principal. We have always agreed that there needs to be room for both of our dreams and ambitions. He was happy and excited to move for my job from California to Pittsburgh and knew that relocations are a given in a retail career, but the timing was totally wrong this time.

The new job offer came after four years as store manager. We were both settling into our careers, loving our house and friends, and our kids were thriving in the neighborhood. Instead of going back to my boss and saying no to the job, I stepped out of my comfort zone and said I would do the job if I could do it from Pittsburgh. To my complete surprise, he said yes and was extremely supportive in making it work. I thought this was a great solution. I could continue doing what I loved to do and the family wouldn't be uprooted. In retrospect, there was an alternative. I could have said no and stayed on in Pittsburgh as the store manager for a few more years.

But back then I didn't have the awareness. My thought process didn't include reflections, talking to people I trusted, and looking at it from a more holistic perspective. I was very interested in what I could accomplish in that job and knew that I would make it all work.

No one forced me to make the decision. I chose myself and later realized how this decision impacted not only me but also everyone in my life. Think about that when you are faced with a similar situation and have to make a decision. So many aspects of our daily lives are the result of decisions that we are responsible for. Have you said yes to a job with an hour commute each way? Have you decided to buy a house a little more expensive than you really can afford? Have you said yes to being the president of the parent association at the school? Have you taken on extra tasks, or were you forced into it? I would say the answer is pretty much always that you made the decision.

In my life and probably also yours, that little word—Y-E-S—is often the villain. It is a great art to be able to say no. I have the tendency to jump up and say yes every time there's an opportunity, but my instinctive reaction isn't always the best idea.

A FLEXIBLE CULTURE

There may not be such a thing as work-life balance, but there are decisions we need to make and priorities to set every day to create a personal balance, and companies need to do their part as well and provide a modern, flexible work culture. This is the only way companies can be successful in the long run.

While I, at times, have been a poor example of creating a good internal balance, it has always been a priority for me to create exactly that for the employees.

When I became HR manager for IKEA North America, the company was growing and needed people to grow, and to take on more responsibilities and bigger jobs. Many truly talented coworkers felt that they could not take on more because they were already feeling stressed in the jobs they were in at the time.

If you need to produce, deliver, and be effective in your job, it is important for there to be a supportive, flexible culture. It can make a world of difference being able to meet fifteen minutes later so you can manage to drop off your child at school before showing up at work.

As a company, we always talked about people being our most important resource, but at the time, we needed to take an honest look at whether our actions were really living up to that noble idea.

We didn't have an HR strategy for North America at the time and there was no HR organization in place to support a growing, successful business. We knew IKEA had a reputation for doing a lot for women, but when I was a store manager, I was one of the very few female managers at that level, and there were no women above me.

My shift to Human Resources management came very naturally. After four years as a store manager, I wasn't tired of the job but saw the opportunities. For me it wasn't just taking on a job; I was driven by the mission of creating a better everyday life for my many coworkers.

In those years, I learned to create strategies and get the necessary support for them, and I knew the importance of implementation. Our strategy had its starting point in the consideration of the whole life of the employees not just the work aspect. We introduced, among many other new benefits, flextime, part-time management positions, job sharing, condensed workweeks, full benefits to part-time employees, and possibilities for people in certain positions to work from home.

Health insurance was a major topic of discussion nationwide at the time. Spouses and children received coverage, but not life partners. If you were living in a gay relationship or you had lived for years together in a heterosexual relationship without official marriage, your partner was not covered. We decided that a life partner should have the same status as a spouse if they had lived together for a specific period of time.

In addition to my responsibilities for HR in North America, I was involved in a global plan. At that time, there was no global HR manager, and our CEO formed a group of HR managers from different countries and IKEA organizations that reported to the executive management team. I was chairperson of the group, and we were tasked to create a human resource strategy for all of IKEA. The strategy became about unleashing the potential of our employees and removing barriers. It included diversity, life balance programs, transparency around job openings, and a strong focus on training and leadership development.

The global strategy was implemented all over the IKEA world and created healthy discussions both internally and externally.

A TURNING POINT

Ironically, I was deeply involved in these subjects in exactly the years where I didn't have any balance in my own life.

We were honored as one of the best employers on many lists, in prestigious magazines like *Forbes*, and I was named the first female Family Champion for *Working Mother* magazine in 2003.

In many ways, my time as HR manager for North America was a turning point, not just in my career but also in my personal life. I was on a huge learning curve, but I got so much experience and accomplished big things, and looking in the rearview mirror, significant changes came from this period. I had proven to myself and the organization that I had potential and could deliver results with the right people around me. But I also learned the hard way that if you're not careful about prioritizing and taking care of yourself, you can end up lying in an ambulance reflecting on whether what you've achieved is really success.

DON'T OVERLOAD YOUR PLATE

My own story has taught me that flexible work arrangements are great and necessary in today's world, but even with the best setups and support, we can still lose control, lose ourselves, and go down with stress. Better benefits and flexible hours do not in themselves create balance. We are each responsible for our own lives. If we overload our plates with too many things, we know something will drop to the floor.

A few years after my anxiety attack, I gained new insights and a new approach to everyday life and prioritizing. Some days it all goes to hell, and other days everything goes really well. Some periods I have to focus on work, while other periods, like when my father was very sick and died, it is all about the personal life.

When I have big projects at work, I focus on them for a period, and if my husband says that in the next few months he will be involved in negotiations and working on teacher contracts and knows he will be busy, I prioritize my work less and family more.

You can't put your private life up on the one end of the scale and your work life up on the other and create a permanent balance. You can't separate the two things. They are interdependent. You live only one life, and you are one individual person.

You are best off accepting that permanent balance is an impossible goal and instead reviewing your life on an ongoing basis. Learn how to prioritize what is important and what you need to take out of your life, give less focus to, or just put on hold.

You can actually manage your life by not just choosing more all the time, but taking things off your plate as well. I have become slightly better over the years, but it requires a constant awareness. In a lot of ways, the panic attack and learning that came from it prepared me for my job being responsible for IKEA North America. I prioritized, set boundaries, delegated, and became better at saying no—all in order to not lose myself again. As an example, I started meetings at ten with a goal of finishing by four. This way, people could catch up on emails, on phone calls, and with staff before or after sitting in a meeting all day. I planned bigger events, when people had to travel, in the middle of the week so no one had to leave the family on a Sunday night or come home late Friday night or Saturday morning. These small changes made a big difference in my daily life as well as the daily lives of the people around me, and there were no real business reasons to start Monday morning at 8 AM anyway.

In that role, there are, of course, always a lot of things to attend to all the time, but some of them are not important. For example, we had an incredible number of business events and guests, and there was a tradition of going out to eat with people visiting. When I stopped that tradition, guests were pleased they had the evening free to explore Philadelphia or just relax, and my team and I, all traveling a lot, were just happy to be home with our families. This set an example for others that it was okay for them to do the same. It actually can be easy to say no; we just have to think about it.

NO MORE MOVES

Some of yeses I have given over the course of my career have impacted not only me, but also my husband and my children. Each time I was offered a new, exciting job, there was either relocation or traveling involved.

Our first move was from California to Pittsburgh when I was store manager. The children adjusted well and ended up loving Pittsburgh, and my husband finished his master's and doctorate and started his very successful career in education. When I took the job as HR manager for North America, it was not the right time for the family to move at all, so I started a long commute from Pittsburgh to Philadelphia for four years.

After a total of nine years in Pittsburgh, my husband actually suggested we move to Philadelphia. He got a great job as a principal for a high school, and everything looked like it was working for us. I no longer needed to be away from home and we both had great jobs. When we went to look at houses, I was called in for a meeting with my boss, the president for IKEA North America at the time. I had no idea what the reason could be and thought, of course, that something had gone terribly wrong. When I arrived, he said that he had been talking with the CEO for the IKEA Group, and they would very much like me to take over and be the president for North America.

I was totally shocked. My first reaction was, "What are you talking about?" After everything I had been through on a personal level, I was finally feeling at a good place in my job as HR manager. I was totally unprepared for this and overwhelmed. To be offered this great new opportunity and challenge was just not something I had ever imagined—it meant we didn't have to move again, as the job was based in Philadelphia. My husband was waiting outside in the car. And as we were driving back to Pittsburgh, he looked at me with a big question mark, as if he was asking, *So?*

It was difficult to process. We both had new and exciting challenges in the same city. How could we have asked for more? It seemed completely unreal, and I will never forget the drive back, five hours of trying to grasp what had just happened. It was like everything had fallen into place. Our one concern was the kids. They wanted to stay in Pittsburgh—we are all serious Steeler fans to this day. Of course, the kids were happy that I did not have to travel quite so much, and they had really good friends living in Philadelphia. They adjusted very well, but it took time. They really loved Pittsburgh and still do today. We were really unaware at the time what Pittsburgh means to us all. We don't regret the move to Philadelphia, but it gave us respect for how hard it is to pull up roots—especially for children.

After nine years in Philadelphia, where my husband's career really had taken off, in 2009 he was offered a great job at the progressive and well-recognized private school the University of Chicago Laboratory School. I was so excited for him, and this time, it worked for all of us to move to Chicago. During a spring break vacation a few years earlier, we had all agreed that it would be a great city to live in.

Just a few months earlier, I had agreed to take on the global HR role. After over eight years being responsible for North America, the job was coming to an end. I had accomplished my tasks, and the organization was set for a new era with a new type of leadership—and I was ready for a change. After many discussions with my boss, the CEO of IKEA, I accepted the exciting responsibility as HR manager for 130,000 employees. There was just one little snag. The position was located in Helsingborg, Sweden. With my history of moving the family or being away from home for a long time, this was obviously a problem.

I decided to say yes to the job but no to moving to Sweden. I didn't want to move to Europe and didn't even want to ask my husband to move. My whole side of the family lives in the United States, so that was not an incentive.

It was during this that I realized that you can actually achieve more than you may think when you dare to say no. It turned out that my boss was more interested in me taking the job as a global HR manager than me moving to Helsingborg. It was okay for him that I was living in the United States. The agreement was that I would do the job for a couple years and see how it went. It turned out to be a good decision not to move to Helsingborg for many reasons, one being the position moved to Amsterdam a year later and the other that we could move to Chicago for my husband's new job. For my job, it didn't matter if I was in Philadelphia or Chicago.

CONSCIOUSLY UNBALANCED

The astute reader can probably still hear the alarm bells ringing. Because while I had declined to move the family to Europe and been allowed to do the job from the United States, both with great success, I had again agreed to travel. In many ways it was the exact same situation as when I chose to stay in Pittsburgh and work in Philadelphia. My domestic commute by air had been replaced with travel to Europe almost weekly.

A key difference was that this time I made the decision much more consciously and with a very realistic sense of the fact that it was not a sustainable way of living and working. I also knew that my life at IKEA most likely would be over had I said no.

As much as I knew my season was probably over, at the time, I wasn't ready to take the consequences of that. Even though it was far from an optimal situation, this opportunity gave me a couple years to do a very exciting job and at the same time consider what was next.

I could work from home when I wasn't in Europe. For the first time in many years, I was able to work at home, without any colleagues, and that gave me a taste of transitioning to a new life.

MORE IMBALANCE AT THE TOP

When I made the decision to take on two more years and lots of trips to Europe, I was forty-nine. I had reached a point in my life where I could rest more in myself, and with that, I felt good about the next couple years. With everything I have experienced through my career, I am humbled by what it takes for women to reach the top and have a good life, but it's possible.

All the barriers that good HR plans and development programs can eliminate for many employees have to be eliminated by women at the top themselves. If top positions were different, many more women would take top jobs. If you arrive there as the only woman, you are the one who has to make the changes. I do not think it is so much about breaking through the glass ceiling as it is changing the atmosphere and the work climate at the top and for those in management positions.

In many companies it is, after all, a man's world with a man's agenda, and that is not a thriving culture for most women. I have met many amazing women who have said no to participating in the typical corporate culture in boardrooms and have started their own companies, where they decide the rules of the game and are able to have quite a different relationship between career and family. Many highly competent women disappear from the big corporations that need precisely their talent. They just don't feel it is the place to be and the sacrifice of not being yourself is not worth it.

The higher up in the system you go, the harder it is to get it all to come together. Men are used to giving things up in certain areas of their life. Perhaps they come home late and don't always get to say good night to their children. Men typically grow up with more goal-oriented decisions about what they want to do and be, and how much money they will earn. For many years, it has simply been a condition for men that they earn money and are less visible on the domestic front.

That choice is relatively new to women, and we are not always good at deciding and speaking up. We are not as clear as the men. We tend to be unclear, more hesitant and confused about what we want. We perhaps aren't ready to give up the influence and power of the home.

In my view, the question is not about whether you are born to be a leader, but whether you want to be one. You must be prepared for hard work—not just a thirty-seven-hour workweek. You will need to take some things off your overflowing plate, and constantly make choices and live with their consequences.

If, however, you are passionate and go after what you want, it doesn't matter if you work sixty hours a week for a couple years. If you start your own business, you are prepared to work millions of hours, because you are working on something you love.

TOOL

THE DIFFICULT ART OF SAYING NO

One of my great sources of inspiration, Oriah Mountain Dreamer, writes in *The Dance*:

"I have sent you my invitation, the note inscribed on the palm of my hand by the fire of living. Do not jump up and shout, 'Yes, this is what I want! Let's do it!' Just stand up quietly and dance with me."

When I am asked to do something, it is easier to say yes than no. For people wired like me, we often answer yes out of loyalty and devotion to duty, or because we are flattered. We believe that others expect us to say yes, but often they expect that we will respond honestly.

1. Next time you are faced with a question that requires you to answer yes or no, pause. Don't answer automatically. Take your time and think about what you really want to do.
2. Don't be pressured to make an important decision without time to reflect. Apply the twenty-four-hour rule. Give yourself time. Sleep on it! Clarify for yourself what your needs and requirements are if the answer is yes.
3. If you say no just because you are afraid of new challenges and are complacent, your challenge is to consider saying yes.
4. Saying no to others because you say yes to yourself is a very important step to change a pattern or bad habit. There are no rules here; every situation is different. What is important is that you make conscious choices and are honest with yourself and others.

Part 4

THE POWER OF NETWORKING AND MENTORING

"It's our light, not our darkness that most frightens us."

—Marianne Williamson, *Return to Love*

11

MEN—EYES WIDE OPEN

I remember when I had just been offered the job as head of IKEA North America, and my predecessor first made the announcement during a breakfast staff meeting at corporate headquarters. He informed the group that he was moving back to Sweden and it had been decided who would be his successor. Everyone automatically looked at the men standing next to him. When he said my name, I heard several gasps in the room. I can only imagine that some thought it was fantastic and others were wondering, *What the hell is this?*

I don't think this was necessarily because I am a woman. Even though I have often been the only woman in a male-dominated world, I have rarely felt that I have been looked down upon or disrespected for that reason. But when I stood there, assigned to a huge job and responsibility for IKEA's most ambitious expansion ever, it was not just because I was experienced, competent, and ambitious, and had the skills and qualifications for the job. I stood there also because the people, the men at the top, had noticed me.

As men sit at the top of most organizations these days, it is important to find ways to include them in the discussions about gender balance and why it is critical for long-term business success. They must open their eyes, engage, see the amazing talent out there, and make a commitment to include women at all levels of the organization.

It's a much-debated topic, and there are many explanations for why women give up along the way. For me, there are three critical factors. First, our own lack of confidence and clarity about what we want. Second, the environment and culture at the top are not designed for women. Third, too few men are really interested and committed to making this a priority.

LEARN FROM MEN

When it comes to confidence, we can be inspired by men. They might only have 60 percent of the qualifications for a job, but they apply as though they have 100 percent. I have also found men to be clearer about what they want to accomplish and just go after it. In my work world and my circle of friends, I see many women who want to do something more, take the next step, but they often have not communicated what they want and are just waiting to be noticed and asked.

Instead of being frustrated about not getting what you want and blaming others, you should take life in your own hands, be clear on what you want, and go after that.

That's one of the most important lessons we can learn from men. Women are wired differently in our brains and for many years, we have been brought up differently, so in general, men are more goal and action oriented. They seem to easily decide what they want, communicate it, and go after it. Of course they can be unsure and confused, but they tend to move on more quickly. If we want more out of our lives, and we want to be more engaged in meaningful jobs and top-level positions, we need to decide and go after our dreams with confidence.

Again, I believe we have something to gain from men, just as there are many things they can learn from us. We can be inspired and learn without assimilating and taking on a role that's not one we are comfortable with. We certainly don't have to try and "become" a man and violate our feminine side, but we can be inspired by men's focus and clear direction and become focused in our own lives. It's about being street smart and learning from others what might work for us.

As I hear it from men, they are often confused about what women really want and about how they can support us. I know that there are times when I expect my husband or a boss to just read my mind, but how stupid and unrealistic is that? I often hear from male colleagues and friends that they want to solve problems and help, but they just don't know how. So by being more specific both at home and at work, we can do ourselves a big favor. My experience is when I am clear and ask for something very specific, it is usually met with "Okay," "That's possible," or "Yes, I can do that."

Let yourself be inspired by the men who for many years have played golf, had their after-work beer, their football, their investment groups, and so on. They have found time even with a busy work schedule and kids at home—time for what is important for them. If they have more time than the working moms for these things, we should ask ourselves: Whose fault is that? Women have always had networking groups in our lives, ranging from close girlfriends and other moms at school to book clubs and walking groups, etc., so we know how to get together and be with each other. Maybe we just need to use these existing networks more purposely or create new ones.

CHANGE THE CULTURE NOW

Another important explanation about the lack of women in the boardroom and at the executive level is that the work culture and agenda have, for decades, been created for men, by men. Most women simply don't find this particularly inspiring and easy to thrive in.

I have met many talented, competent, ambitious women who do not want to be part of this environment at the top. Many have also told me that they could not even imagine doing what I do because there is so much pressure and stress. These jobs can be made much more attractive to women, but it requires that we change the culture at the top by creating a more inclusive, open, creative atmosphere with time on the agenda for discussion and brain storming. There needs to be honesty, transparency, and a culture where all opinions are valued and respected, and where leaders are involved and truly listen to the team.

In my view, women are less interested than men in having a job for the purposes of prestige and power. Of course, there are many women who want to have power and influence, but in general, women are more interested in solving problems, in collaboration, and in dialogues than in the actual power; more interested in improvement and development than in the results and the bottom line. I am one of them. Companies could have more of both if there were a better mix of men and women in key positions. So yes, it is important to break the glass ceiling, but even more important to change the discussion and the culture at the top to see real, sustainable change happen.

I believe more women would be interested in top positions if they could see that it can be fun, inspiring, exciting, and challenging to be a leader—if we can show more good examples, so people can look to this and say yes, I want to be part of this.

I am very aware that these changes don't happen overnight.

Personally, I even found it difficult to change the culture and the agenda in my own meetings, where I was in charge. To be respected, I certainly had to prove I knew what I was doing and talking about, and even then it was still difficult, because the system and existing setup had been that way for years. I did manage to make some changes. I created a different meeting structure, created time for open discussions and different meeting times—but it was difficult, and it met lots of resistance. With my own experience in mind, I can understand why it has been so difficult to significantly change the number of women at the top of the business world—and why the women who are there in spite of it all have not yet paved the way for more sustained change.

I have been part of many teams and a few boards where I have been the only woman, and I have at times found it extremely challenging to get my voice heard. For years, I was beating myself up for not communicating clearly enough, for being too vocal, or for not speaking the same language only to find out other lonely rangers like me experienced the exact same thing. It was a huge relief and breath of fresh air when a second woman joined, and then, when a third came on board, I felt we were making significant contributions and starting to effect real change. There is a saying: one is a token, two is a conspiracy, and three is a breakthrough. I was part of IKEA's executive team for over ten years and can confirm that this was exactly my experience and have examples from being one, two, and three.

The most memorable moment was when our third woman joined. She had worked for IKEA for many years and was so excited to be part of this team. I shared with her that the culture and atmosphere were different than in most other places in the company—quite intense, competitive, and challenging. During her first meeting, we went through a quite complicated project, and the presenter went very fast, not even trying to give her background or context. She at some point asked, "Could you slow down and speak a little slower?" A colleague looked at her with frustration and told her to learn to listen faster. Needless to say, she was quite upset after her first meeting. We decided to change the tone in the room after that, and it did change over time. The real breakthroughs come only when women seriously use their voice and influence to implement significant changes.

I have many examples of great, diverse teams I have been part of where we had tough but supportive discussions, shared lots of ideas, and made some really critical decisions. Usually, strong leaders who valued and respected everyone's input and contributions facilitated these teams. My board jobs with both Save the Children, US and International, are good examples of strong leadership and very productive, effective, and inspiring meetings. Both boards have such diversity and outstanding people from different aspects of society and the world.

MEN HAVE TO SEE THE LIGHT

What a pity for all the companies missing out on incredible talent because the men in charge don't get it.

Several studies point to the benefits of a diverse distribution of age, race, and gender within companies, such as higher revenue, expanded number of customers, and greater creativity. According to the US nonprofit organization Catalyst's latest study, which followed *Forbes*'s top five hundred firms over five years, companies with more than three women on the board have better financial performance than those with fewer than three.

Let me share a handful of very thought-provoking numbers.

According to the US Department of Education, women make up 50 percent of the population, over 50 percent of college degrees, 60 percent of master's degrees, 45 percent of MBAs, and in 2009 women held more PhDs than men. Over 70 percent of all buying decisions are made by women. According to a US Department of Labor Statistics study done in 2009, 50 percent of all middle management positions in Fortune 500 companies have been filled by women since the 1980s. Yet over the last thirty years, the percentage of women advancing to senior management has remained low. According to the Grant Thornton International Business Report, in 2010, only 15 percent of those who made it to the executive level were women, which is an almost insignificant change from 14 percent in 1996, and only 3 percent of CEOs were women, with no change in that number since 1996. It is difficult for me to comprehend why getting more women in executive positions, as CEOs, and on boards is not a priority for any modern leader today. Most of these areas have experienced enormous developments in the past thirty years. But somehow, diversity at the top is really stuck and clearly not due to lack of talent.

As individuals, we have lots to do ourselves to be clear on what we want, to prepare ourselves for new responsibilities, and to speak up—but that is just not enough. At some point, the responsibility for change rests with those who actually have formal power. The light needs to go on at the top, and as most companies and organizations are run by, as Governor Ann Richards put it, "a thick layer of white men," it's those men who need to engage and take ownership.

There are, of course, many who take it seriously and see this untapped potential as a great business opportunity. Once they make it a strategic priority, it's amazing how quickly things can change. Kenneth Chenault, CEO of American Express, and Paul Polman, CEO of Unilever, are good examples, but they are too few. Both of them as leaders of global businesses have made a commitment to diversity because it is good for business and it adds value to their organizations. They are focusing on a diverse, global customer base and American Express has put gender intelligence on its strategic agenda to develop its business. Both Chenault and Polman have focused on these issues and achieved great results in a very short period of time.

A SHORTAGE OF CONFIDENCE

One of my very close colleagues told me many times that he had come to realize how lucky he is—lucky because he is a man, born at the right moment in time in progressive Sweden. He has had many different big jobs at IKEA and was HR manager for Canada when I first met him.

If you ask him, he will confirm that the top jobs in the business world are the domain of men. He has worked for decades developing numerous programs around leadership, diversity, and personal development, and he has facilitated hundreds of programs and met thousands of people. It took years for him to truly understand how the conditions and challenges for women in business are so different than those for men.

At one point, I asked him to help create and facilitate the program I & IKEA, which I mentioned earlier. I simply could not understand why so many successful, strong businesswomen had suddenly, at least in their own minds, reached their limits. Time and time again, I experienced female middle managers and executives who started questioning themselves, doubted their abilities, and became insecure.

It shocked me how long it took for many of the women to get ahold of and discover their personal strength and power and start building their confidence back.

We had them ask themelves, and you can ask yourself the same: "Why do I think negative thoughts about myself and my abilities? Why do I give myself permission to erode my confidence? Why not focus on what I am good at, what I am proud of, and my accomplishments?"

I have met and worked with many female leaders from different parts of the world, and I realize our insecurities and lack of self-confidence are often our biggest obstacles. We need to believe in ourselves to follow our big dreams. Of course, the workplace must have an environment and policies of flexibility for women with children—and fathers who also have increasing needs and requirements. But it is my experience that it is not the practical challenges of balancing job and personal life that cause women to give up on their careers. Instead, it is often a lack of support and acknowledgment from bosses and colleagues, and a lack of trust.

We worked with I & IKEA for over a year, and it took months before the participants dared to discuss the many obstacles that were self-created. The acknowledgment is necessary before you can begin work to remove them.

In the years following, my colleague lead a number of informal sessions as part of I & IKEA. He has since told me that before the program began, he thought he had a good understanding of women and how we work, think, and are, but I & IKEA showed him things he never would've considered. Though he now feels more educated, at the same time, he admits that he is still an amateur in the field and is humbled by the topic "women, leadership, and women's needs on the job." He has great respect for what women think and go through, and how little men know about it. It is a bit of a depressing picture of the insight men have when a progressive man like my colleague, who has spent decades working with people and the subject, feels he knows so little.

Of course, it doesn't take a long time for men to understand, but it is necessary to sincerely listen to women if they want to find out what it takes to make women satisfied and successful at work. As long as more men don't open their ears, it is unfortunately a reality that many women won't have the desire to participate at the top.

WHO WANTS TO WORK SEVENTY HOURS?

Setting quotas is, of course, a possibility, and it has worked in some countries, but in my opinion, it can only be a solution if everything else fails. Success and progress can come from the CEO and leadership team setting clear goals and expectations—backed with full commitment. Lasting change requires company-wide commitment and a genuine willingness to transform things.

It requires that both men and women see the benefits and recognize the need for an updated work culture, one that works for both men and women. More female executives and a more modern working environment can certainly be a win for men too. Who really loves to work seventy hours a week and be available twenty-four hours a day? Who invented that? What good does that do anyone?

If you have a job that you can't handle within reasonable working hours, in my opinion, you need to question whether or not you are a good leader. What specifically constitutes reasonable working hours depends very much on the culture and the industry you work in. But I believe that if you constantly work more than fifty hours a week, it is either a sign of doing something wrong, being a poor leader who can't delegate, or having a leader who delegates but doesn't provide the necessary resources for the tasks to get done. If you are good at organizing, delegating, and assigning people who are accountable for the problems and crises, you do not need to be involved in making all the decisions.

There are many opinions and assumptions about work culture in the executive suite, and I know many qualified and competent women who have decided the culture is not for them and have chosen to start their own businesses instead. There's no question in my mind that the intensity at the executive level is high by nature. Considering that, it is still possible to make it more inclusive, collaborative, interactive, and open to new ideas, and this is where women can and have a responsibility to contribute. For sustainable change, it is not enough to break the glass ceiling. It is necessary to challenge and change the traditional work practices and adjust some of the entrenched structures and habits. Does an executive management meeting need to run until eight o'clock at night? Everyone can benefit from setting a hard end time. Does every meeting need to be packed with a tight agenda with no time for quality discussions and meaningful interactions? Experience has taught me that when you make a big personal decision, you have the opportunity to create a new beginning.

I once had a senior manager who had difficulty making it in on time in the morning, but could stay later. This issue was solved very simply by implementing more flexible work hours and some time working from home. A similar example comes from my own life, when I was allowed to remain in the United States, even though my job was situated in Europe. We have a responsibility to ourselves and others to ask and be part of creating a new, modern environment. Who says things should remain the way they have been for the last fifty years? Who says you can't achieve what you want? Take yourself seriously and figure out what works best for you.

CHOOSE YOUR HUSBAND WITH CARE

Be aware that your partner or spouse plays a big role in your career. I would never have been able to do what I have done without the incredible support of my husband for twenty-five years. For us, it has been important to make it clear to ourselves and to each other what our values and ambitions were. Although we come from different backgrounds—he grew up in a Mexican American family in California—he always knew I wouldn't be the one at home doing laundry, cleaning, and baking.

Conversely, he has also been very clear that he wanted to be the best father he could imagine. So for him it was always okay to be the primary parent. He was certainly also the one who was best suited for it. When we had our daughter, my dad actually commented that there was more mother in my husband than in me.

Our starting point has always been that we never stop each other from doing what we want. My husband is eight years younger than me, and I have always earned more. From the very beginning, our setup has been quite unique. If anyone asks, he answers with comfort that his wife earns more than he does. We have been clear from the outset, have talked about it constantly, and, in connection with the book, I asked him again how he saw our model for juggling two careers and a family.

When working on this chapter, I asked him to share his version of our relationship and the way we organize our lives. Here's what he wrote:

Our life together began as a friendship, and that has always been the starting point for everything we have done. We have supported each other as great friends and always focused on what the other needed to be happy and satisfied. This does not mean that it has always been perfect. We've both had our share of mistakes, been selfish and shortsighted, as most people are occasionally. But in the end, we always know that we will do everything to help each other, and that's why we sleep well at night. We fit well together because Pernille has always known that she wanted to be successful in business and make a difference by addressing challenges in the retail industry, particularly in relation to people. A natural consequence of those challenges has been moving, traveling, and long working hours.

I've always been a teacher. I spend my working hours making the lives of children in school just a bit better. The school is close to our home and it has been a good fit with our own children.

Our interests have complemented each other. Pernille has been forced to travel to an extent that few comprehend. But we have, as a family, benefited from her work financially. It is interesting to note that no one would lift an eyebrow if she had been male. Our roles are reversed, and people around us don't always fully comprehend that. We have both been very lucky to be able to explore our passions, be challenged, and simultaneously feel the support from the home front. Family comes first for both of us, and yet we have had to define our own version of the model. We have not only challenged the general view of what others think "family first" means, but even more so, our way of living has challenged what our own families have found "acceptable."

I think we are really lucky. Pernille has never tried to run from the fact you can't be a mother, career woman, and wife without making choices. She lives in the moment, so when she is with the children and me, she is rarely distracted by other things and is always present. For years now, I have thought our life has been at its peak—we are maintaining it and I am still learning something new all the time, and I feel that we are still growing as a couple. Yes, sorry, it might seem corny. But what could be cornier than a Danish girl from the countryside and a Mexican American city boy who find each other and build a life together?

WOMEN DON'T KNOW EVERYTHING

As my husband says, we are not perfect, but we give room for each other's dreams and passions. I can say with confidence that both privately and on the job, I have met men who have supported me—my husband and incredibly good managers, employees, and colleagues. I feel that the men in my working life have seen me as Pernille, and not just thought, *She's here only because she's a woman.* They have gotten to know me and have valued my contribution. On the other hand, I have also encountered men whom I immediately noticed for some reason or another were not very supportive of me.

For me, it's not about either men or women, but *both* men and women. Men have many refreshing qualities that I need in my life. Both sides can learn something from each other. Sometimes we, as women, need to remember that we are not experts in gender. We have much to learn about ourselves, just like men have, and we sometimes think that we are experts on men and know exactly what they are good at and not good at. One example from the home front: rarely is it the man telling the woman how to be a good mother, but I am willing to guess that most women can't resist formulating what a good father is. We have much to learn about the opposite sex.

I certainly do not want to replace male culture with female culture. I have no ambitions to create a society that is controlled only by women. I am hoping to inspire a truly inclusive environment, where we are on an even playing field, and our differences matter because they are appreciated.

TOOL

GREAT MINDS THINK UNALIKE

This saying comes from my friend and colleague Barbara Annis, an expert in gender intelligence. From my many years working with men and women, it rings so true for me. We each bring our individual uniqueness to the table, but we can't forget that gender adds another dimension as well, and as these differences are understood and appreciated, we create an inclusive culture, where everyone contributes, thrives, and delivers results.

Here are six things to consider as a gender-intelligent leader:

1. Do not make assumptions about the other gender; instead, ask questions.
2. Understand how to take advantage of the strengths men and women bring.
3. Actively encourage collaboration and different perspectives in meetings and in decision making.
4. Treat gender intelligence as a high priority, and seek to learn more and encourage others to do the same.
5. Be highly self-reflective. Actively seek to learn about your impact on others and seek feedback to be more self-aware.
6. Actively promote the presence of both men and women in all situations.

Taking this idea further for each gender, the following are tips for both men and women on working effectively together (which works at home too):

Men

1. Women need ongoing authentic, sincere recognition and appreciation. A simple "Thank you," "Great job," or "How was your weekend?" goes a long way. Most women don't leave a job because of "life balance issues"; they leave because they don't feel valued.

2. We have a need to vent and express our thoughts, feelings, and opinions—and for the most part, we don't need solutions or answers, just an ear.

3. We have a tendency to hold ourselves back, underestimate and undervalue our credentials, and see obstacles rather than the possibilities. We need to be reassured, we need to get support, and sometimes we just need a gentle push.

4. Women bring a different and important perspective. We look at situations through another lens. We read situations and people quite well, and we think of things holistically and tend to think more long-term. Men need to make sure to pay attention to our points of view and include them in important decision-making processes together with other diverse experiences. Including different opinions and experiences leads to better decisions and a more engaged culture.

5. Men get very nervous when women cry. I facilitated a workshop where the men asked for women to please never cry at work. But this is simply how we sometimes express our emotions. Men tend to get angry. If it happens at work or at home, the best thing to do is hand us a Kleenex and ask if we need a minute.

Women

1. Know what you want and need, and don't be afraid to communicate that. If you don't know what you want, no one else will either, and others can't read your mind.
2. Clear, straight-to-the-point communication works. When I'm in meetings with men, I know that thinking while speaking doesn't work. I don't have to be the first to speak. It can be good to take a few minutes to prepare my thoughts clearly.
3. Bring your full, authentic self to work. Stand up for what you believe, express your opinions, and when you meet resistance, don't take it personally and give up. It is important to be comfortable with disagreements. That's all they are.
4. Step out of your comfort zone and take on challenges that scare you a little. Women have a tendency to not pursue important jobs because we don't think we are qualified. Men tend to pursue jobs they are not quite ready for, but they have the confidence.
5. Men have lots of strengths we can learn from. They tend to be more focused on the task at hand, getting to the end result, and making decisions based on solid facts. Find male mentors in your organization or network and create a relationship you can both learn from.

You can learn more about gender intelligence and Barbara's work by going to www.baainc.com.

12

NETWORK—WE ALL NEED CONNECTIONS

I was just back from vacation. It was August 2004 and I was going to Long Beach, California. Before the holiday, I had agreed to speak at a conference hosted by the Women's Leadership Exchange for eight hundred female entrepreneurs.

From the moment I met the network's founders the evening before until the moment I left the conference after lunch the next day, I was part of something special, something that came to open many more doors than I ever could have imagined. Never before had I felt that energy at a conference.

The energy coming from these eight hundred women was contagious; they were sharing with each other, discussing partnerships, and giving ideas. I met several women who I am still friends with today. This group loved IKEA, and they were all using the products in their businesses in a multitude of ways. They inspired me to develop IKEA US's focus on small businesses. I saw the huge business potential. In addition to meeting new friends and getting real business advice and inspiration, I also got connected to two incredible organizations: the Women's Leadership Board at Harvard University and Belizean Grove.

This group and the conference gave me such a boost, both personally and as a businesswoman. I discovered the power of networking. These entrepreneurs had something in common; they didn't seem to see each other as fierce competitors, were sincerely interested in each other's businesses and in supporting each other, and were very committed to creating a healthy economy, new jobs, and spotting new opportunities. There was no question in my mind that this network and the strong connection between these entrepreneurs were both a great personal and business advantage. I was determined to start making networking a much more integral and conscious part of my life.

My mother is a breast cancer survivor and had a long but successful road to recovery. Her fight for survival inspired me to join a total of three different Susan G. Komen Three-Day Walk for the Cure events—each sixty miles in three days. What an experience and personal achievement it was each time! Thousands of women spent three days together marching in the rain through the hills, heat, and city neighborhoods; sleeping in tents and nursing blisters; all to raise money to prevent women from dying of breast cancer and to help raise money to find a cure. It is incredible what women can do together when we have a mission, take charge, and get organized. Spending three days together and meeting hundreds of wonderful women lifted my spirits and made me realize the possibilities.

Think about it. Today there is a whole month dedicated to breast cancer awareness, and we even inspired the tough NFL football players to wear pink the entire month of October. Not all women are angels, and we don't always come together, and sometimes we fail to support each other. Women can be incredibly judgmental of each other, jealous, envious, undermining, and outright mean, but as former Secretary of State Madeleine Albright put it, "There is a special place in hell for women who don't help other women." If we want to change how the world treats women, it starts with how we treat each other.

Both in my professional and personal life, networks have become a key element, and I rely on them all the time. I use them for making decisions about investments, business opportunities, vacation spots, getting inspired, and even just nurturing my confidence and meeting new friends.

I do believe networks need to have a purpose to stay alive and interesting. Some women's network groups have deserved a bad reputation and caused many organizations to avoid them because they became more about bashing and venting than working on something constructive.

SISTER SOLIDARITY!

Throughout my own career, I have experienced and witnessed that the greater and more demanding job you have and the higher you go in the hierarchy, the fewer female colleagues there are to talk to. That is not a good place for us to be. We love to connect, to talk mother to daughter, as sisters, girlfriends, and colleagues. We thrive when we have a solid sense of sisterhood around us.

Formal network groups are a more recent concept. I believe they have emerged from women taking on bigger leadership roles and from the growing need for bringing a form of sisterhood into the workplace, as we have had throughout history outside the workplace. There is something special about meeting a room full of women, in an open and trusting atmosphere, who are facing the same challenges as you.

Besides participating in many different networks, I have also attended many women's conferences with lots of practical take-aways, good examples of what other companies are doing in terms of developing women, and keynote speeches from successful executive women I can learn from. These types of conferences are more about providing input and information, and tend to be less intimate than networks, which provide opportunities for personal contacts and deeper discussions. Belizean Grove is a wonderful network that is a combination of inspiration, gaining new knowledge about relevant socioeconomic issues, leadership, technology, new perspectives on future trends, and at the same time having conversations with friends, drinking wine, getting new cultural experiences, sitting by the pool, or even playing a round of golf. The group consists of women who have all made it to the top in their fields and made a difference. We come together once a year for a long weekend, most recently in Panama. This group of women has meant the world to me, especially when I was lonely at the top. When someone from the group contacts you for anything, it goes to the top of your list of priorities. It is a true sisterhood.

FABULOUS NETWORKS

So I know now that women have a tremendous need to relax with other like-minded people. It's great that there are all these organizations that executives and professionals can join, but you don't need to stand and wait to be invited to join an exclusive club. You can form your own network—large or small.

Let me give you an example. I feel one of the most special and unique relationships we have with another woman is the relationship between mother and daughter. When my daughter had to leave home, we decided that once a year, we would do something together to develop and safeguard our relationship. We started our annual Fabulous Women's Retreat, invited other girlfriends, mothers, and daughters, and formed a new network.

We included our close circle of friends and family; whether they were seventy or sixteen didn't matter. The first time, there were seventeen of us in Florida. My daughter and I were among the last to arrive. The noise level was already high—everybody was talking, introducing each other, and an instant trust and comfort was established. We were together for three days and talked about the very topics I have written about here: deciding what kind of life we want to live. It confirmed to me that there is such incredible value in taking time away to reflect and have a chance to share your concerns, challenges, and passions with others—to both get feedback and confirmation, to get inspired to go back home with renewed energy and an appetite for life.

Many times we just need a secure setting, an open atmosphere with no finger pointing, a place where people listen and where we have the opportunity to listen and learn.

The purpose of the Fabulous Women's Retreat is to work hard, laugh, have great conversations, meet new friends, catch up with old ones, and celebrate with good wine and food. We meet in a beautiful and affordable setting, and we all go home with some goals for the year to come.

When we meet, we discuss all the important areas and challenges in our lives, whether it is about our relationships, our jobs, our health, our family, or something else entirely. The first time we met, we used the Four Rooms of Change model (coming up in chapter 14) to help guide the work and conversation. It is a great practice to assess where I am in different parts of my life, and it makes it relatively easy to realize where I need and want to focus. We spent hours sharing this with each other in smaller groups, and I was just so impressed with the level of honesty and openness these women were expressing and the kind of questions they were asking and the feedback they gave each other as support. The next day, we went on to look at what specific parts of our lives we wanted to change, and then we set specific goals and actions. These were not three-year business plans, but plans for our lives.

I have many examples of concrete changes as a result of those discussions. Last year, one of the participants was very dissatisfied with her work. After our conversations, she realized the cause of her discontent and frustrations was that she could not live with the culture a newly hired manager had created. Suddenly, she was clear. It wasn't her personally; it was the environment that had changed, and she left the weekend feeling powerful, knowing she was ready to make a change. Shortly after, she found a new job. It was not necessarily her dream job, but was a job where she still thrives.

Another participant had a job that had become unbearable, but she couldn't put her finger on why. With the help of the group, she realized it was all because an important relationship with a colleague had gone sour. She went home motivated to address it with her colleague. She took responsibility and is again happy in her job. They didn't truly solve their disagreement, but it no longer took up space in her life.

Women of all ages are getting something out of these retreats. My fifteen-year-old niece attended our very first gathering. She is a great girl, who had a rough time in middle school and part of high school. At our first retreat, she was awarded our first Fabulous Woman Award. The idea behind the award is to encourage the honesty and courage to change; the award goes to the person who, over the weekend, exhibits the most honesty and courage.

On the last night, it was given to my niece to take home as a reminder of the inner strength she had connected with. The figurine is passed on to someone new each year. Unfortunately, my niece couldn't make it the year after, but in handing on the award, she wrote this note:

> Last year I had the great honor of receiving this award. For me it symbolizes great female strength and the ability to find out who we are even when things are at their worst. Over the past year, it has served as my lifeline, a symbol of how all women are important and will support me. It has been a year of ups and downs, but fortunately this powerful symbol reminded me of the promises I made to myself last year. Now it's time to pass it on, but the symbol I carry with me. I stand now as a confident woman, and no matter what challenges life brings, I will always be able to say that I am proud to be who I am. I am me. I am woman!

In many ways, her letter describes what I hope this book will highlight. It is evidence that, if we support each other, we can ignite strong feelings and a powerful force within each of us.

If groups of women met every six months and were to call upon each other in such a way, I'm sure it would create great change and growth. I hope you'll be inspired to establish similar groups or start a blog where you can exchange thoughts and experiences.

MIXED MINGLES

An all-male or all-female network has its purpose and can bring huge value to the individual, but I also want to emphasize the importance of a mixed network, even if it becomes something else. It is often a way to exchange practical experiences and business cards, and discuss current trends and news within specific disciplines. It is a way to get to know a broader business community and to connect with and get to know new male colleagues, which can be extremely beneficial.

Women are really good at networking outside the company. Men are very good at networking inside the company, which is something we can learn from men and cultivate in ourselves. We have a great opportunity in using our external networking skills inside the company to develop connections and relationships across the entire spectrum—gender, ethnicity, level, age, and profession. Mixed networks add another dimension. If you use the women's network for support, building confidence, and feeling empowered, you can use the mixed network to develop professional connections, explore career opportunities, and find mentors and job coaches, both inside and outside the company. And it will help you remember that we also have a few things we can support our male colleagues with as well.

NETWORKS WITH A SOCIAL MISSION

During my time as president, I was fortunate enough to be invited to one of the major humanitarian organizations that IKEA supports, Save the Children, US, and became a board member. I am on my second term and have recently joined the international board as well. I feel extremely honored to be part of this organization and to have an impact on how the world treats children, but I have also built an incredible network of people among the board members and staff.

In Chicago, I have joined the board of a community organization addressing the under-resourced communities in the city. Through this work, I now have a whole new network of people and connections in my community.

As a volunteer for another small nonprofit organization, Spark Ventures, I have become part of its network and met a whole new group of young professional Chicagoans.

If you want to grow at work and in life, I would dare to say that it is not a question of joining a network, but a question of which ones to join.

TOOL

BUILDING NETWORKS

Some of the networks I am a member of are invitation only; others are open. The Fabulous Women's Retreat I created with my daughter started as invitation only. Networks come in all shapes and sizes, from large, prestigious business networks to smaller social groups, where you come together with a specific focus, like books, walking, or golf. It is my experience that women especially have a need for networking, and people to talk to, share with, bounce ideas off of, get inspiration from, and support. You probably already have a few. Look around at your sisters, girlfriends, and colleagues, and there is a huge opportunity to use these groups more consciously.

The Fabulous Women's Retreat is an event that we created to have fun and to have time to reflect, grow, and more importantly, develop deeper relationships with a great group of amazing women.

HOW TO GENERATE YOUR OWN NETWORK/RETREAT

1. What is the purpose? Do you want the network to have a specific theme or goal?
2. Consider who you invite. How will each person contribute? Is each one open to growing and developing? What will the dynamics of the group be?
3. Finding the right place will help set the tone for your retreat. Look for a comfortable place with a good atmosphere. It can be a vacation home, a bed & breakfast, a small hotel, or a spa.

4. Send an invitation where you describe the purpose and get people excited.
5. You want to develop an overall agenda for the days. Know it doesn't take much to get women to open up and share, as long as it is in a trusting and safe environment.
6. Using the "Four Rooms of Change" model can be a great guide (see chapter 14's practice section for how to use this).
7. Discuss also what ground rules you want for your network and what expectations you have. Establish a trust agreement: everything you talk about is confidential and will not go outside the group.
8. Set a time limit for each person to talk when sharing in a group. At the first Fabulous Women's Retreat, I forgot to do that, and as a result, one person in one of the groups took up all the time. No one felt comfortable enough to step in, because no ground rules were communicated.
9. Keep everyone focused on the person whose turn it is to share.
10. Learn to listen. Use your ears more than your mouth. Listen to what is being said without preparing a response, passing judgment, or providing automatic advice. Instead, ask open-ended questions.
11. Before parting, each person prepares and shares a plan for action based on the discussions during the retreat. What will you redesign in your life?
12. You want to end with a reflection of the retreat. Ask the group what they got out of the time and what can be different in the future.
13. Set a date for your next retreat and decide on how you will keep in touch in between. You can create a Facebook group.

14. Use each other as mentors/mentees as a follow-up. See the next chapter, as well as its practice section, which is designed to help with selecting and being a mentor.

13

MENTORING—LESSONS IN THE ART OF LIVING

"If you want to travel fast, travel alone;
if you want to travel far, travel together."

—African proverb

When I look back at my life, I can see I have always had a certain sense of confidence in myself that I can trace back to my parents. They have given me many gifts, but the one I cherish the most is this unwavering confidence and support. I have had lots of crazy ideas, and my father especially always supported me in the things I really wanted to do. I have met many people who have not been so lucky. One of my bosses had his own theory: that behind a strong and confident woman is a very supportive father, and behind a frustrated, angry man is a very critical dad. I know from mentoring hundreds of people, facilitating lots of workshops, and bringing up two kids of my own that parental support, confidence, and commitment have a huge impact on who we are as adults. I have also come to understand the concept of mentoring and that my parents were my first mentors. From the day I was born, they have, as Zalmon Schachter-Shalomi says, "imparted lessons in the art of living."

We all need someone to believe in us and support us, and as human beings, we develop best when we grow in the presence of those who have gone before. If you weren't brought up with parents nurturing your confidence and guiding you in life, it can certainly be a disadvantage and make it all that much harder to find the way. It becomes then even more important to find the support of others.

Networks are one avenue to find support at a more personal level and get a mentor. It was not until late in my life that I even became aware of the concept and realized that I have always had mentors in my life and informally mentored hundreds of people.

It was around 2000, I was HR manager for North America at the time, and we wanted to develop a mentoring program for IKEA. We were about seven HR experts around a table, and we all had completely different views on what mentoring really is. For two days, we looked at different existing programs and best practices, discussed definitions, and started outlining our own version—but we got stuck. We realized we were not experts and finally listened to our most senior person, who for two days had been trying to say that we didn't know how to do it, but she knew someone who could help us. This person had just published a mentoring guide, and her philosophy fit perfectly with our culture. Because of this, my friendship with Lois Zachary started. Together with her, we developed a successful mentoring program, and she has informally been a mentor for me for almost fifteen years.

As the old African proverb says: if we want to travel far, we have to travel together. Lois believes that is mentoring at its core: to travel far together in a relationship of mutual learning. She believes everything that happens to us is our teacher, and as adults, our best way to learn is through critical reflections on experiences.

I have often been asked who my own mentor is, typically with the expectation that I would mention some well-known businessperson. The truth is that there is never just one mentor in our lives. There are several different ones at different times. The idea of mentoring fits very naturally with the idea of designing the life you want to live, constantly reflecting on what is happening, and deciding how to move forward and figure out what to focus on. Artist Brian Andreas expresses it well: "Most people don't know that there are angels whose only job is to make sure you don't get too comfortable and fall asleep and miss your life."

My longest and most valuable mentoring relationship has been with a more senior, older colleague. He knows me very well, I trust him, and he always gets me to see new things, challenges my thinking, and asks me simple but thought-provoking questions, and I leave every conversation with a feeling of renewal, a new perspective, and a great sense of connection. I know I give him a number of things as well. He speaks about very complex concepts, and I ask him to make it practical. I am an ear for his new thoughts and latest discoveries. He gets an opportunity to share what he is working on, and we challenge each other to constantly have new insights.

He helped me recognize that my anxiety attack was a great gift, that being approximately right is better than dead wrong, that I needed to stay away from other people's hurricanes, and that every thought I have is either shrinking or expanding and it is in my control.

Trust is the foundation of a good mentoring relationship, and it also has to be built on open and honest communication, authentic dialogue, and a good connection. To have someone you can call upon in your personal and professional life, someone to rely on when you are having disagreements with your boss, considering a promotion, facing a layoff, or are thinking about starting a family is so important. Many books are written about effective mentoring relationships. Lois has already published at least three books that are guides to getting the best out of such a relationship. The take-away today: everyone needs a mentor; and to pay it forward and develop, everyone needs to mentor at least one other person. Set expectations for the relationship, discuss ground rules, establish goals, and have honest, meaningful conversations.

WHO CAN BE YOUR MENTOR?

Your spouse or partner may be good to talk to about a lot of things, or a sibling, parent, or friend can be good, as you can use the mentoring concept in any conversation or relationship. In different periods, I have had meaningful mentoring conversations with my mother, my sister, my brother, and my girlfriends.

My closest friends and I have taken turns helping each other with problems over the years. One time I will do the asking, and the next time it is my friend. As my children have become teenagers and then adults, they have also been mentors in my life. I have asked them their views on jobs I was considering, and they asked me questions; my daughter even challenges me when she sees me being passive-aggressive with someone. They ask me the exact same questions I ask people when I am mentoring. Teenagers and young adults can be brutally honest, and you know they are usually right on. They may not have the years behind them, but they have insights and are not at all afraid to tell you what others may not dare to bring up.

These conversations are great, but from my experience, if you really want to grow, it is important to have someone who is not too involved in your everyday life, who can look at things without emotion and give you an outside-in perspective. I am sure there are people in your life who are great candidates. At work, I would look for someone you trust, feel a connection to, have something in common with, can imagine will challenge you; someone older, more experienced, and who has already had experiences like the ones you are currently facing. Once you find someone, don't be afraid to ask. I know I am always honored and flattered when someone approaches me. I have mentored colleagues from different parts of the IKEA organization, start-up CEOs, women facing career and family questions, a neighbor, my husband's colleague's wife, and a totally confused twenty-five-year-old MBA graduate.

In 2009, just after I was appointed global HR manager and had moved to Chicago, I was asked to speak at a women's conference in Miami for about eight hundred people about business opportunities in a declining economy. A few weeks before the conference, my new boss asked me to be at a meeting in Amsterdam on that day; he *needed* me there, he said.

I contacted the organizers and told them the bad news, but they didn't take no for an answer and arranged for a live video speech from the offices in Amsterdam. In the audence that day was a young woman from Chicago. She liked my views, and the day after, I received an email from her asking if I would meet her when I was back in Chicago. I thought: *Wow, that is personal leadership*. I said yes. We met a few weeks later, and I have mentored her now for almost four years—about everything from quitting a job she hated and negotiating salary, to handling stress and life beyond a career fast track; she also comes to the Fabulous Women's Retreat.

I remember the first meeting very clearly—she talked for almost two hours without a break. She had so much on her mind. My first advice to her was to get a journal and write in it daily for three weeks. "Let's meet again after that," I told her, but at the same time, I really wasn't sure I could expect to hear from her again. But she called, we met, and she had told me that she had realized through her journaling that she had to quit her job.

One of my challenging and most gratifying mentoring relationships is with our "adopted son." He came into our lives when he was in high school and dated our daughter in Philadelphia almost six years ago. He had a tough upbringing and saw a college basketball career as the only way to a successful life. My husband and I have been his mentors and "parents" through a demanding and stressful life at college. We have had the tough life talks and been part of the disillusions, the bad decisions, and the many ups and downs along the way. He is learning and growing from us, but even more importantly, my husband and I are learning as much from him—mostly about ourselves. He will graduate soon and has more opportunities than just basketball.

LISTEN TO YOURSELF

If you do not have someone in your life whom you can trust, whom you can be honest with, and whom you have constructive conversations with, you probably need to first look at why that is. Secondly, you may need to look harder and in a broader circle.

Another option is to use yourself. I have learned over the years to critically reflect on what is happening in my life. In addition to having mentors, I have learned to be my own mentor.

I am sure you have experienced just how easy it is to advise others on what they should do. You give your friend some good advice, and a few months later, she can give you that same exact advice. I can't tell you how many times I have said to myself, "Maybe I need consider using the advice I just gave."

When we are accused of not being good listeners, it most likely starts with not being good at listening to ourselves. My amazing and sweet friend can sometimes call and talk for forty-five minutes. She often finishes by saying, "Great talking to you, honey. I've got to go." She hangs up and I have hardly said a word!

Sometimes we talk a lot or make ourselves very busy to deflect from ourselves and to avoid looking inside. The last few years, I have used all I have learned and practiced with others on myself. I take a step back, distance myself, and look at what is happening. How I am feeling? Where do I need to focus? The ability is built over time based on my own experiences. You have the same.

I certainly became much more conscious when I started to work on myself after my anxiety attack. I'm not so sure that other people saw the change, because it was happening inside. Both personally and professionally, I started to notice signals and signs, which to this day I continue to pay attention to. When I wake up in the morning, I can immediately sense what is going on with me. It may be a trip I am anxious about, a relationship that is bothering me, or one of the kids I am worried about. I can very quickly zoom in, accept it, and address it. If I face a conflict or a problem, I am okay to let it stay there for a while, until I find the right solution. Before, I would rush to find a solution, and most of the time, it wasn't the right one. I have more patience, and pay more attention to myself and my surroundings.

I have always felt that I have given a lot to others and have spontaneously been available to help and give good advice. The question is what really was my intention behind all of that. Sometimes I probably did it without even being asked and without reflecting on what was really happening—and maybe without really listening. Instead of focusing on myself, it has been easier to be the one who automatically just help others. My intention has primarily been to support others and their needs—but underlying that, it might have been a way to avoid focusing on myself.

Becoming better at listening to myself has not changed who I am, but it has given me some important and useful skills, and an increased awareness that helps me mentor myself.

The way we sit in a chair is a good picture of how we relate to life. Rather than leaning forward, ready to jump up, I try to tell myself that sometimes it is okay if I lean back and just listen, rather than participating in the discussion or taking on a job. I am better about sitting back, listening a little more, to myself, my body, and other people.

AN ONGOING PROCESS

It's comforting to know that I can use myself in that way. In some sense, it's like having money in the bank. It provides a reassuring feeling that I can draw on my experiences when I hit a bump in the road, but it doesn't come by itself. Self-development is indeed a constant process and hard work. The work is never done.

New challenges continue to emerge in my life. The first months after we moved to Chicago in 2009, I felt a little overwhelmed. I coached myself and said, "Pernille, your daughter has left home and started college." It affected me much more than I had imagined. It was really a big change for me that she was no longer in our lives every day. Suddenly she was gone, and I probably had not really noticed how I truly felt about it.

In addition, I had a new job, my husband had a new job, my son had just started his junior year in a new high school, and we were looking for a new place to live. No wonder I was feeling a little off balance.

When I found the *why*, I could accept it, and I gave myself a year to adjust to all the changes. I had to take it one day at a time. I mentored myself, and my journal was, as always, my best guide. I don't need to write much to see a pattern. Just a few years before, I would not have come to the realization so quickly.

It is important for me to emphasize that I didn't wake up one day having mastered everything. It is a long process, and I am still working on it. Know that it is hard work, but it is well worth it. Many of these things can't be fixed once and for all. The reality is that much of what we each struggle with is part of our own construction, and therefore, we must make small and ongoing changes.

You can't expect to be looking out through the window today and see something completely different tomorrow. Focus on the small steps and changes. Your consciousness can similarly change, and you are able to see things in another way. If you have already been through a major process of developing yourself, you do not necessarily need others to provide you with questions that get to the heart of the matter. If you work consciously with yourself as a mentor or use someone else, you can speed this development up a bit. We all need to have our own experiences to really learn, but there is nothing that says you have to take as long as I have.

After I moved to Chicago and worked from home much of the time, I mentored myself more than ever. It was necessary, because I had no colleagues or bosses around me all the time. I was alone, although I traveled to Europe almost every week. It wasn't long before I could sense that I wasn't feeling quite right, so I started journaling almost daily. Pretty soon, I could see what was popping up again and again. I felt I was never at the right place at the right time. I never had enough time at home, or with my staff, my colleagues, or my boss. People literally asked me if they could have a second with me, so in addition to never being at the right place at the right time, all my relationships were stressed by too little time.

The conclusion was very clear to me, so when I went to my annual development talk with my boss in Holland, I knew the time had come. After we finished the conversation about how the job was going, it was time for me to share that my time at IKEA was over. And that was the start of my next trip . . .

TOOL

SELECT A MENTOR AND BE A MENTOR

It is important to have a mentor by your side as you design the life you want to live.

Not everybody is part of a formal network or has been assigned a mentor through their work, so you will have to take charge yourself and select your own mentor. I would guess you already have a few mentoring relationships in your life. I am talking about people you trust, ask for advice, and look to for guidance but whom you may not have thought about as mentors. Selecting a mentor more consciously can speed up your development and progress.

1. You don't have to hire a professional mentor. Look around among the people in your life and list three possible candidates. Consider someone not involved in your everyday life (spouse, partner, parents, boss), who has experienced what you are going through, who is maybe older, someone you can trust, who is a good listener, and whom you have a natural connection with. It doesn't need to be someone you know well—a little distance from your life may actually be effective. Once you have three names, prioritize them based on what you want to use the mentor for.

2. Clarify for yourself why you want a mentor and what you want the mentor to support you with. It can be career focused or about your relationship with your spouse, your health, or your wellness. I have a friend of a friend who asked if I would be a mentor and help him get clarity about his business and how to take it forward. He also asked if, when he had that sorted out, I could

support him in looking at his personal life. It was very straight-forward. I knew I could support him, and I said yes. Once you are clear on what you need, don't hesitate to make the connection and ask. Most people will be happy to help.

3. Once you have selected a mentor, you have to develop expecta-tions, set a goal for the outcome, and determine the frequency of your conversations together. It's very important that you take charge of the relationship and the follow-up.

4. We all can be mentors as well. I have many mentors in my life, and I, in return, mentor numerous people. Each relationship teaches both parties, and I bring what I learn from my mentors into my own mentoring role and have become better over time. This is a great way of giving back, unleashing others' potential, and creating new relations. My eighteen-year-old niece, who is in college, is, together with some of her classmates, mentoring eighth grade girls from a poor, underserved neighborhood in Chicago.

5. As a mentor, the main responsibility is to provide support and guidance, share experiences, ask questions, and listen.

6. Posing the right questions will get to the essence of what is important. If your mentee is not getting along with the boss, there are lots of questions to ask in order to uncover the reasons behind the poor relationship. Use factual questions, like: "What happened? Why did you disagree with the boss? Take the situa-tion apart and find out what really happened. When did things start going wrong?" That can take away some of the drama and will help the mentee to understand how he/she arrived at "my boss doesn't understand me."

Part 5

MY JOURNEY CONTINUES

"The boy told himself that, on the way toward realizing his own Personal Legend, he had learned all he needed to know, and had experienced everything he might have dreamed of."

—Paulo Coelho, *The Alchemist*

14

AT A CROSSROADS

Dear friends and colleagues,

I want to share with you that I have decided to leave IKEA. This has been a very difficult decision to come to after twenty-one fantastic years. As I have advised and spoken about for years, there is no such thing as work-life balance; there is only one life, and it is about making decisions every day. Now I need to follow my own advice and be realistic about my life.

I am fortunate to have had such an incredible time at IKEA, and I have had more opportunities than I ever could have imagined when I left Denmark at twenty-three to be a young entrepreneur in the United States. My potential at IKEA has been unleashed. I have developed both personally and professionally because of IKEA and all the supportive people I have been fortunate to be around, including you. I am truly blessed and thankful. My kids grew up with Mom working at IKEA, and they have a great life, partly because of that. My husband reminds me that I have been married to IKEA as long as I have been married to him.

When I accepted this great challenge as global HR manager two and a half years ago, I was not ready to leave IKEA. I was committed to continuing to contribute to the development of IKEA as a company and, as always, to growing personally with new dimensions. For personal reasons, I did not move to Europe at the time and have been fully supported in all aspects in commuting from the United States. As a family, we have our life in the United States. My husband has been an amazingly supportive partner during my IKEA career, and we have moved a few times—to great benefits for the whole family. He has developed a successful career in education, and with both of my kids wanting to go to college in the United States, we will continue our lives here. After two and a half years of commuting every other week—sometimes every week—over the Atlantic, never feeling I was in the right place at the right time, and never having quality time for anybody, including myself, it's time to accept reality and make a decision. It is not a sustainable life for me, or the position, and you deserve much more.

It is with sadness, pride, and a warm heart that I officially part with the company, but IKEA—the spirit and all of you—will always be a big part of who I am. With humbleness, I thank you for that.

It is a glorious future!
Pernille

I left IKEA in the summer of 2011, and the decision to leave the company is one of the biggest I've ever made. It was very emotional, and I imagine that it's a bit like getting divorced. For many years, IKEA was such an important part of my life and gave my family a great sense of security. I had been the main provider, and all of a sudden that changed.

I had come to an important crossroads, and I had to be honest with myself and face the fact that it no longer worked. The decision had to do with courage, values, my compass, and everything I've learned about myself.

After two years as global HR manager, what I had known deep inside when I took the job became crystal clear: it was not a life I wanted to live. I couldn't continue to live in Chicago and travel to Europe every other week. I have always traveled a lot, and for the most part enjoyed it, as I loved my job. Being responsible for North America, I was mostly traveling with my colleagues, visiting and opening stores. Now I found myself in a job where traveling to Europe by myself almost weekly was part of everyday life. I was traveling just to attend meetings and do my job.

This setup also meant that I never really could travel to meet the different organizations around the world and be an inspiring, effective HR manager. I was spending all my time just getting back and forth. It boiled down to the idea that, for the second time in my career, I could not be fully present in any one location. I wasn't home enough, I wasn't at the office enough, and I wasn't out in the organization enough—a setup and solution I was solely responsible for.

I was committed to making it work for at least a couple years. As always, I wanted to live up to my own and others' expectations—and deliver what I promised—so I made constant adjustments and looked at how much could be done via Skype and video conferencing. However, IKEA was still working in a more traditional way, and meeting face-to-face was an important part of the culture. Six months into the job, I got a new boss who decided to have executive meetings once a month in Amsterdam from Thursday morning to Friday lunch. That was a reasonable plan, but for me it was a huge adjustment, as all the other weeks I had meetings with my own team in Sweden, other HR managers from around the world, and key line managers. I learned to find every possible flight that would bring me back to Chicago Friday night.

As a very experienced traveler, I can sleep on any plane and don't suffer from jet lag, but there is still seven hours' time difference, and it takes a toll on you over time. It just was not a sustainable way of working—for me, my family, or IKEA.

I was heading down a familiar path—that of the Energizer bunny that just goes on and on without any breaks. Maybe I could have persuaded my husband to move to Europe, but I knew it wasn't the right solution for any of us.

WHEN TIME IS UP

There were lots of other aspects of IKEA that had changed over the few years before I left. There were new priorities, a new agenda, and more streamlining, and as the company had gotten so much bigger, I also had to face that there was less need for entrepreneurship and new thinking. My job as global HR manager was completely different than being a line manager with profit and loss responsibilities and my own organization. When I reflected on my values in relation to my job, I realized that three of them—trust, courage, and passion—were fading away. Commitment was the only thing still standing strong.

There was nothing especially wrong with IKEA. It was different, yes, but I didn't have the feeling that everything was better five years before. I had reached a place in my life and a place at IKEA where I had to make a decision. I had achieved more than I had ever imagined. I had been part of the executive team for over ten years while still managing to live in the United States. I have realized over the years that I do not thrive in an environment of maintenance and status quo. Challenges, changes, and driving new initiatives energize me. I have never chosen the easy route when I have taken on new jobs. Most of the time, I have thrown myself into something completely new, where, of course, I have been able to draw on my experience. My passion for new ideas and new ways of doing things wasn't needed so much anymore—and maybe my ideas were not so new anymore either.

My jobs haven't just been about me, Pernille, but they have been a great combination of my leadership style, my strength, and IKEA's ambitions and priorities. My assignments have aligned nicely with my leadership, skills, and passion *and* with the specific business tasks. I have always felt that, in addition to what's important to the company—including embracing the strong corporate culture—there has still been plenty of room to express who I am and what I stand for.

I had a fantastic career at IKEA, a career that I never could have imagined. This doesn't mean that I haven't had ambitions. Of course I have. You don't live a life like mine without ambitions, but the way I have interpreted *ambition* has been to constantly improve. Titles have never been the driver for me. The motivation has always been the opportunity to do something new, make a difference, and have the possibility of creating change. I had reached as far as I wanted to and what was possible at IKEA.

At the same time, I had arrived at a point where everything I worked on personally had given me a new platform to stand on. I had more confidence in who I am, and I had invaluable insight and experiences that I hadn't had ten years ago. IKEA and my colleagues taught me so much, and I have become aware that it is just as important to develop as a person as it is to continue to get better at the professional aspect of my life.

I had come to a place where I wanted to live a holistic life aligned with my values, desires, and ambitions. Naturally, I had considered if there were any alternatives to leaving, and my new boss was very willing to find another solution, but it had become crystal clear. It was time to move on. My season at IKEA was over.

TOOL

LIVE THE LIFE YOU DREAM ABOUT

The Four Rooms of Change is a very useful practice to help us embrace the constant changes in our lives. It has been a helpful friend for me, together with my journal, for many years. I wrote earlier that you have a profound influence on living the life you want, and growing and feeling in control, strong, and happy. With new knowledge, insight, and strength, you can get beyond any challenge, struggle, or problem, but it doesn't happen by itself. It is work on your part and requires a willingness to take an honest look at the different aspects of your life and be prepared to address certain things. We cannot control everything that happens to us, but we can control our response.

Here is my own version and explanation of the Four Rooms of Change, inspired by physiologist and author Claes Janssen's model.

ROOM OF CONTENTMENT

I am happy and content. My most essential needs are covered. I am okay. I am free of jealousy and don't compare myself to others. Everything is fine. I have no need for changes.

ROOM OF SELF-CENSORSHIP

Something has changed. Perhaps a sudden loss, death, sickness, or being fired has turned my life upside down. I ignore the signals and pretend that everything is still okay.

I am not okay and things are not good. I am worried, uncertain, and uncomfortable. I deny the truth. I don't talk about it. I can't bear to face the problems. I behave like a victim and communicate with negative vibes. I am passive-aggressive. I defend and hang on to the past and am not open to change.

ROOM OF CONFUSION AND CHAOS

I have reached the point of collapse. I finally accept the way things are. I dare to expose all the ugliness to the light. I accept that it is natural to go through a hard period and that conflicts are a natural part of life.

I am angry and confused. Uncomfortable feelings from the past appear. I am letting go of the old constructions I had created in my head about myself or a relationship, a job, my financial consumption, my unhealthy lifestyle, etc. I am overwhelmed but am beginning to see a solution. I am ready for change.

Our culture hasn't prepared us for confusion; we are taught to be okay. But this room is the most important. This is where the big changes happen. It is not a particularly pleasant place to be. But it is important that you give yourself plenty of time and not rush. Hold out through the discomfort, and the answers will come.

ROOM OF INSPIRATION

I put everything behind me; I feel honest, connected to and close to the real me.

I can manage it! I can reach my goal. I have a plan. I know what I want and what I have a need for. I feel inspired and like a new person—full of energy, on top, and strong, and I can't wait to get going. I am ready for change.

Once the honeymoon is over, I throw myself into the new, start the job, realize the new possibilities, and deliver my plan. I move back into the Room of Contentment.

HOW TO USE THE FOUR ROOMS OF CHANGE

Look at the different parts of your life: family, relationships, jobs, school, finances, health, lifestyle, your personal well-being, and so forth.

Place each part in the room that you feel it belongs in.

I have found that the room of self-censorship is the most challenging, so be really honest with yourself. "Most of us are denying something, saying "no" to our true selves, rather than "yes." But once you name it and place it, you are already on the way out."

As you place things in the different rooms, consider:

ROOM OF CONTENTMENT

Things that are under control, working well, are okay, and that you are satisfied with—these aspects of your life don't require any change at the moment.

ROOM OF SELF-CENSORSHIP

Everything that drains your energy, things that you don't dare be open about. The things that you don't feel comfortable talking about, are trying to avoid and ignore. The things that you hope just go away or will get better with time.

ROOM OF CONFUSION

The things that you're a little hesitant about and that you do not know how to move forward or what to do with. Things that frustrate you and that don't have a solution. Anything that raises a lot of questions but has no answers just yet.

ROOM OF INSPIRATION

Everything that gives you a feeling of excitement, makes you smile, helps you feel completely free of worries, and energizes you.

When you have placed all components of your life in the different rooms, start working with this information:

1. What do you want to move? What do you want to focus on? Look at the parts of your life that are in the Confusion Room or in the Self-Censorship Room. Much of your anxiety and unhappiness are often hanging out in these rooms.

2. Share your Four Rooms of Change placement and thoughts with someone you really trust, a friend or a mentor. Be open to feedback and ask him or her to be honest.

3. Decide on two things you want to address and commit yourself to doing something about them. As a start, you can decide on one topic that is in Self-Censorship or Confusion Room and one from the Contentment or Inspiration Room.

4. Set realistic goals and make an action plan with small steps and important milestones. It's better to start slowly, be realistic, and achieve results, even if they're small, than to have big, goals you will not achieve right out of the gate.

5. Use your journal for this work and make sure to follow up to keep the process going.

A&L Partners AB holds all rights, immaterial and material, to the Four Rooms of Change theory, concepts models, analytical instruments, and Claes Janssen's text. Claes Janssen psychologist, researcher, and author is the originator of the Four Rooms of Change. The Four Rooms of Change is a registered trademark and may only be used by certified users and other individuals with written permission from A&L Partners AB. If you are interested in learning more about the Four Rooms of Change, the Conflict between NO and YES, Claes Janssen works, or to become a certified user, write to info@fourrooms.com and in the subject line write Permission Request or Certification Program.

15

POWERFUL POSITIONS—REDEFINED SUCCESS AND STRENGTH

Now what? I was standing there, having said good-bye to a very exciting twenty-one-year career with IKEA, the world's largest home furnishings company, and a great job with HR responsibilities for 135,000 employees. If you had asked me five years prior, that exact scenario probably would have created a feeling of emptiness and uncertainty about the future, a sense of having lost an important part of my identity.

I felt stronger than ever before, although I had no idea what I would be doing in the future. It certainly helped that the decision had had time to simmer and sink in over time, and most importantly, the decision was based on my own compass. The feeling of strength and the sense of power—even when faced with a completely unknown future—was a milestone in my personal journey, and I hope it has inspired you. Instead of the end, I saw new opportunities and a new beginning—a new path to venture down.

I had reached the point where a powerful position in life can be defined in new terms. For some, it may be sitting in executive management of IKEA for ten years, as I had done. It could be as CEO for the North American business or global HR manager, but not necessarily. Success for me was no longer just about a powerful executive position. For me, success is when you are deeply grounded in who you are—when you are connected to your own personal power and potential, and are prepared to handle anything that comes your way without losing yourself. It is when you finally want to be the person you really are, when you make decisions that will continue to move you in the direction you have decided, and when you have the courage to say no.

REDEFINE SUCCESS

Most of us tend to be very narrow in our definitions of success, power, and strength. These are often associated with climbing the career ladder, earning more and more money, and having more and more titles. That is the way society and expectations have conditioned us. Our "success" is typically connected with our job, our position, how important we are in the business world, how much money we earn, and with the visible, materialistic symbols to support it.

A while back, I was approached by a headhunter from a well-known search firm who wanted to talk to me about several possibilities as CEO, HR manager, and other executive positions for a number of the firm's big clients. It was flattering and tempting, and he was even talking about chauffeurs and traveling by private jets. But after some time of reflection, it just didn't appeal to me.

I would be lying if I said I have not been driven in my career. It has meant a lot to me to have important positions with influence. I'm proud of what I have done over the years, the changes I have driven, and I am proud of the glass ceilings I have broken through—and the few I have shattered. I have done some things that no woman did before me. I am proud of the potential I have been part of unleashing, the people whose development I've supported and whom I have challenged to take on new responsibilities. I have made plenty of mistakes and could certainly have done many things differently, but I have learned and grown from these experiences. I have been given huge responsibilities with different positions, and I feel I have lived up to my own and others' expectations.

I'm proud when I look back, but that isn't what guides me into the future. I have learned that there is more to life than just work and career. I have ambitions to live a life now with slightly different priorities. Like in the book *The Dance*, I can be still and quietly say, "I am happy. I am content. I have a wonderful life." It's a very powerful place to be.

This isn't to say you shouldn't pursue an exciting, challenging job. But it's actually not that hard to achieve. To create a life where you are happy, satisfied, and resting in who you are, where you are emotionally strong and confident, and have a big heart for yourself and others is a much more difficult journey than getting a powerful job with a fancy title.

I have made a very interesting observation. If you do the work with yourself, take that personal journey, feel self-confidence and personal power, and are comfortable in your own skin, it is much easier to get the job you want and to perform it well. You can be yourself. You know who you are, what you like, what is important to you, and what will not work. You have the courage and insight to say yes or no. On the other hand, if you have not worked with yourself, you can easily wander, restless and discontent, from job to job, because you have never taken the time to stop and reflect on what you really want in your life.

My message is of course not that you need to do yoga, write in a journal, meditate, and be happy while the world passes you by. I hope that it encourages you to know that you can be more aware of how to achieve success in life by going beyond the purely professional, step-by-step career plan. I hope that you have also had the opportunity to see that there is another angle on success and how to get to a successful place in your life. Maybe that involves a big job—maybe it is bigger than you ever dreamed of.

TOOL

BE YOUR OWN MENTOR

Try using the Four Rooms of Change:

1. Be realistic about how much change you can take on all at once. Don't have expectations that are too high and that you can't deliver on. Take the pressure off yourself by setting small, realistic goals.
2. Take a few hours to write down what you would like to change in the next six months—whether it's personally, at work, family-wise, or in other parts of your life. Look at them again after six months, and see if the changes have happened simply because you wrote them down and became conscious of them—I bet they did!
3. Adjust the goals as needed and use your skills as a mentor. When I wake up in the morning, I notice whether I feel calm, relaxed, anxious, or worried. I can feel it in my stomach, and I keep asking myself questions until I get to the root of my worry. Once I know what is really bothering me, I can start adjusting and take action.
4. Make it a point to develop your consciousness over time. Let it be your guide. I have developed mine through different experiences, by working with myself, journaling, reading books on the subject, and through yoga and meditation. In yoga and meditation, you work very consciously on the concept of stepping outside your head and observing the thoughts coming to you.
5. I believe we can all learn to use our awareness. It is a very powerful practice to use in a variety of situations—especially when

making decisions. If you have a plate in front of you with unhealthy but tasty food, using your awareness, you will stop for a second before you dive in.

6. Some type of routine is important. It's easy to forget about writing in your journal or going to yoga. Whatever you decide to do to sharpen your awareness—whether it's meditation, journaling, yoga, or workshops—try to be consistent in doing it.

7. Questions I ask myself periodically:

   Have I been in this situation before?

   Have I lost the connection to my values or my passion?

   How much time am I investing in myself right now?

16

COMING UP FOR AIR

The first day of my new independence was, fittingly, July 4. The executive team, together with our spouses, had had a wonderful celebration in Stockholm after our last meeting.

Stockholm in the summer is one of the most beautiful places in the world, so it was a memorable setting to say good-bye in and a perfect date to start the rest of my life. The fourth of July will always have a special meaning for me—it became my very own independence day.

Following my departure from IKEA, my biggest goal was to take a year off and learn to do nothing. With my personality and energy, this was hard work, as you can imagine, and a bigger challenge than an intense agenda with a to-do list a mile long. I decided on a few guidelines for myself for the first year, so I wouldn't quickly be back in a job or with a whole new set of responsibilities, because the open space was uncomfortable. I decided not to pursue any new jobs or discuss opportunities for at least eight months. I committed to writing in my journal for the first one hundred days, and I wanted to stay at home in Chicago to discover the city I loved but hadn't had the time to explore—and to spend time with my husband.

I was overdue for this time. The first many weeks and few months, I felt relaxed and calm, and most significantly, I enjoyed the incredible sense of freedom. For the first time in many years, I could wake up in the morning with absolutely no agenda and take a few hours to drink coffee, read the paper, and watch the morning news. It felt like an extended vacation, but without the Sunday blues that evening before heading back to work.

My first real test of "doing nothing" came after the first summer, when the fall arrived and everybody went back to their jobs and school. I was suddenly hit by an inexplicable Lutheran feeling of guilt and the urge to ask myself, "Is this really all right? Maybe I should consider getting a job again. Maybe I'll be forgotten if I don't get started again and stay visible and relevant."

Thank God for the other voice saying, "This is what you promised yourself. You have worked hard for this and given the appropriate amount of time. New answers will come." My journal helped me a lot through this period of time in my life—I saw the pattern quickly and stayed the course.

LEARNING TO BE NOBODY

What we do and where we work is a big part of our identity, and when you peel away those layers and take away the job title, we might suddenly feel naked and insignificant. For so many years, I had been somebody. As a colleague put it after his retirement, now I had to learn to be nobody. I liked that idea and embraced it.

When I was out or at an event, I presented myself just as Pernille Lopez. If anyone asked, I simply said that I had quit my job and was taking a break. Saying it out loud was surprisingly easy and freeing. My own and other people's reactions actually surprised me. Somewhere I probably feared that people would look at me strangely. But I usually got a high five followed by congratulations—"way to go," "cool," "bravo," and other positive responses.

At the same time, I have also been surprised by how many times we are asked for our title, current employer, and yearly income. Every time I had to leave all the spaces blank, I was confronted with the little voice and I had to convince myself I was doing the right thing. It was a little humbling when I was not qualified to cosign my son's lease without an income, without a job, and without an employer.

My toughest challenge was not making any money. Ever since I was thirteen years old, I had made money. Now I was feeling a little nervous that I was not getting a salary each month. It was a crazy feeling, because I knew we had prepared well, I'd done enough, and this was temporary. Despite all the good arguments, I still occasionally felt guilty for not contributing and did not like the feeling of dependence.

THE HUMBLE NEW LEARNER

As someone who has always prided herself on being a lifelong learner and student of life, I still had never imagined how difficult and inspiring it would be to allow myself to be a humble new learner. I must say I have found myself in surprising new learning situations in this time-out—from learning the art of doing nothing to swimming.

Swim lessons reminded me that we often have to take a step back if we want to move forward. If we want to be better at something or change something in our lives, we have to step out of our comfort zones and dare to be beginners again. Going to my first class in a bathing suit, with cap and goggles, and swimming as a ten-year-old was humbling.

For some time I had dreamed of doing a minitriathlon. After realizing my ability to swim would not be sufficient for making it in Lake Michigan, I started to take lessons. I quickly got the strokes right and slowly but surely became fitter and faster, but the breathing was a terrible struggle. My coach kept giving tips, but it didn't seem to help. One day, he realized my problem. "You are trying to get to the other end without breathing and that will not get you better. You have to breathe, come up for air."

I told him that this had been my problem the last twenty-plus years. I had not been breathing properly. I did not come up for air. This was my biggest aha moment that first year, though certainly not the last.

Another humbling experience was walking into my first Bikram class. I realized that even though I had done yoga for many years, here I was truly a beginner. I learned to stay calm in heat, and I mean 107 degrees with 40 percent humidity. I learned that twenty-six poses are different every day, even if you have done them your whole life—because we are different every day. And I learned that every time we have worked hard and extended ourselves, we have to take a break and rest.

When I started my two-week intensive Spanish course, I learned quickly how much of a beginner I really was, even with the many long vacations over the years to Mexico, and it reminded me how hard it is for me to learn a new language. This was worse than swimming like a ten-year-old. After two weeks of class every day, I still couldn't hold a conversation with a five-year-old.

Learning new things is humbling but also invigorating, and it adds new dimensions to our life. I will always be a student and want to learn new things, but I have a whole new respect for what it takes starting as a beginner at fifty-four.

DESIGNING MY OWN LIFE

So here I am. I haven't climbed the Himalayas, haven't traveled around the world, and haven't yet learned to speak Spanish fluently, but I have slowed down. I have simplified my life, and now I spend time appreciating the things that really mean something to me.

I had expected that maybe after eight months, I would have a clear picture, a new drawing of my life, but still, after a few years, it is just starting to emerge.

I know I want to give back in the form of board work, humanitarian work, mentoring, and facilitating empowering workshops for people who want to take responsibility for their lives and grow. I know I want to work with entrepreneurs and maybe start my own business. I have reconnected with my love for writing, and I want to have lots of time for friends, family, and good food. I want health, beauty, and nature.

So designing my life continues. I am living my very own advice, and it is much easier to tell others what to do—that I know by now.

TOOL

DEFINE YOUR OWN SUCCESS

1. What does success mean to you?
2. What will it take for you to feel successful?
3. What must be fulfilled in your job and your life to give you the feeling of happiness and satisfaction?
4. Once you have defined your personal success, are you investing just as much time and energy in that as you have in planning your career?
5. Do you feel prepared to handle anything that comes your way?
6. If you are spending too much effort thinking, Why can't I be a little more like her over there? turn it around and say, "Why don't you just want to be the person you are?"

Say to yourself, "I'm good enough. I am who I am, and that's good enough."

Let go of the illusions and embrace your imperfection with all its beautiful flaws.

EPILOGUE: LIFE COMES FULL CIRCLE

"Until one is committed, there is hesitancy, the chance to draw
back . . . Concerning all acts of initiative (and creation), there is one
elementary truth, the ignorance of which kills countless ideas and splendid
plans: that the moment one definitely commits oneself, then Providence
moves too. All sorts of things occur to help one that would otherwise never
have occurred. A whole stream of events issues from the decision, raising in
one's favor all manner of unforeseen incidents and meetings and material
assistance, which no man could have dreamed would have come his way.
Whatever you can do, or dream you can, begin it. Boldness has genius,
power, and magic in it. Begin it now."

—William Hutchison Murray, Scottish mountaineer and writer

"**B**oldness has genius, power, and magic in it. Begin it now." These words move through my mind as my husband and I roll down the highway. It's June 14, 2014, and we're on the road again, this time heading west for our next chapter to unfold, back to California, where we started together twenty-five years ago, returning for my husband to head up a school in Southern California, and for me to continue my freelance work, which I can do from anywhere. Our daughter has finished college in Los Angeles and decided to stay, and our son moved out to join her a year ago—needless to say, we are happy to all be in close proximity.

Over 2,200 miles lie ahead of us, the car packed with what we need for the next few months, and our life in Chicago and the city skyline are behind us. Our furniture is in storage, waiting to join us at some time in the future—we don't know quite where or when. It's a strange but invigorating feeling. I am the navigator again. I have done the detailed planning this time. We have three stops: Kansas City, Kansas; Amarillo, Texas; and Flagstaff, Arizona.

It was twenty-one years ago that we left Los Angeles for my job in Pittsburgh with two young children and a world full of possibilities and an unknown future. So many treasures have been collected along the way: some incredible experiences, adventures, friendships, failures, and successes, and maybe most importantly, we have discovered what matters in life.

It's been three years since I left IKEA without a plan for what would be next. At the time, it seemed like such a big decision, and now when I reflect back, yes, it was a significant change, but I feel even stronger today—it was the right one. I had no idea what I would be doing, and I am so glad I took the first year off and didn't make any commitments. I have designed a life that fits me today and includes the elements I am passionate about, but it took longer than I had expected, and there have been times when I was quite confused and impatient.

On several occasions, I have been tempted to jump into exciting projects and organizations with both feet, and at times I just forgot everything I have learned and jumped up and said yes, when it really needed to be a NO! The good thing is I knew this was going to happen and caught myself in time before I beat myself up about it. It happens to everyone. We repeat the same mistakes sometimes and follow the same unproductive patterns. To design the lives we really want to live takes time and hard work, and includes bumps and detours along the way, but it's exactly these bumps and detours that give us the insights and lessons we need in order to move forward toward our goals, missions, and personal legends.

So now I am on two corporate boards, one in the United States and one in Denmark. They are both great organizations, both in retail and both big grocery businesses, which is new to me, but a fascinating world to be part of. I like my board responsibilities. I can contribute, support, and challenge and in return, I learn from my board colleagues and the executive teams. I have become very involved with Save the Children both in the United States and internationally. In addition to being a trustee, I chair different committees and get involved where my experience can be of value. It's a big time commitment, but the mission "to save children's lives, to fight for their rights and help them fulfill their potential" is inspiring and motivating.

I continue to coach and mentor, especially young women and entrepreneurs—both formally through leadership institutes and informally through personal connections. I was excited a few months ago when I got a LinkedIn request from a young women in Denmark, who had read the original Danish edition of my book and felt compelled to get to know me and have me as her mentor as she was taking on a really big career challenge. I have also coached three young entrepreneurs while their company has moved from a small start-up with a technical platform for furniture design to reinventing the entire product development process, and they are now ready to sign contracts with some big, well-known furniture companies.

I continue to facilitate workshops and retreats and will do more of that in the years to come. In February we celebrated our fifth annual Fabulous Women's Retreat with record attendance, and with *Design Your Life* being out now, I have a great platform to build from. I can feel the idea of building something ignite my entrepreneurial spirit. I don't know exactly what this means yet, but I am good with that, because sometimes being bold and brave is just sitting still, taking it in and doing nothing. The answer will come.

Like William Hutchison Murray says in the quote above, you have to dream that you can do and then do. And buckle up, because boldness is rewarded. If there's one thing I want to leave you with, it's this.

Be bold and brave.
Take charge of your happiness.
Design the life you want to live.

I can't wait to connect with all you "life designers" out there and hear your stories.

ACKNOWLEDGMENTS

If it weren't for you, Susanne Svendsen, publishing director of Gads Forlag in Copenhagen, and your persistence for over two years, I would not have written this book. Thank you for your leadership, your vision, and for pushing me out of my comfort zone. Thank you, Karin, for being the real writer behind my story. I am most thankful for the friendship we have developed through this project, and I look forward to continuing to develop our vision. Thank you to my friend, Cynthia Black, cofounder of Beyond Words Publishing, who is sadly not here to read the work she initiated. We met through Belizean Grove, and she said from the day we met that one day she would publish my book. She kept her word. Thank you, Jason, for your incredible support and love through the last twenty-five years—anything worthwhile is hard work. Here's to our next chapter! Thank you, Mom, for your unconditional love and trust and for letting me do all the crazy things most daughters don't do. Thank you, Mette, my big sister, for watching out for me not just as toddlers, but throughout over lives together. Soren, I can't thank you enough for being my brother, best friend, and business coach these first years in the United States. I wouldn't be here if it weren't for you. Thank you, Malene, my little sister for letting me test out all my crazy ideas on you and not telling. Thank you, Hanne, for being my friend for a lifetime. Thank you for reminding me at the age of ten to stay true to who I am. Thank you, Hansy, business partner and wonderful friend. We did what most people will never dream of. Yes, it didn't go quite as planned, but the experience and friendship I wouldn't dare be without. Jens Rask, thank you for the emotional, financial, and professional support you and Lois gave me during my start-up years in Fort Lauderdale. You always knew I was going to make it. Thank you, Ulf, my dear friend, colleague, and mentor. Your presence has had a tremendous impact on my life. I am forever grateful. Anders, my daring, radical, and trusting boss, thank you for giving me challenges way beyond what I believed I could do and for never losing confidence in me. Thank you, Lene, Paget, and Sari, for creating a huge relief by letting go of perfection and instead celebrating "mothers of imperfection." Thank you, Sten, Jan, and John, for giving me opportunities that made a significant difference in my life. Thank you, Kim, Michelle, and Kippin, for being fabulous, loving stand-in moms. You made our lives possible. Thank you, Calvin, for coming into our lives. You are truly living the essence of this book, overcoming your many challenges and obstacles and designing your life. Thank you to all the amazing women I have met all over the world, to all my dear friends and colleagues, and to my families on both sides. Thank you, Sine, and thank you, Sebastian, for every day making me realize that I am a pretty good mom after all.

APPENDIX: FURTHER READING FOR YOUR JOURNEY

Books and poems have always inspired me. When I look back, I have used different kinds of books depending on what I needed at the time. I started out with very specific management books when I got my first management position. As I became more experienced and started to develop as a leader, I chose books that could help me identify who I am as a person and what I stand for. Here are some of the books that I have used along my leadership journey:

The One Minute Manager by Ken Blanchard
It gave me support and practical tools to focus on when I was green as a new manager in my twenties. My uncertainty and lack of experience made it important to learn the basics of being a manager, both of the business and the employees.

The 7 Habits of Highly Effective People by Stephen Covey
This book came in handy when I was a little more experienced and eager to improve. It helped me understand how to prioritize, do the right things, and see the big picture. I became more effective and aware of the impact I had on my surroundings.

On Becoming a Leader and *Managing People Is Like Herding Cats* by
   Warren Bennis
These two books opened my eyes to leadership not being about keeping it all together and having full control, but instead about letting go of things, delegating, and giving people freedom. With an environment where employees feel their opinions count, they

can take ownership and feel involved, and together we can accomplish big things.

The Four Agreements by don Miguel Ruiz
This personal development book inspired me a great deal once I had become a more experienced leader. By becoming more aware of who I am and what I stand for, I became a more conscious leader. It is not the end goal but more a milestone, a new beginning.

The Dance by Oriah Mountain Dreamer
Oriah and her book have helped me accept who I am, both the good and the bad—to be proud and encourage others to do the same.

The Art of Possibility: Transforming Professional and Personal Life by
    Rosamund Stone Zander and Benjamin Zander
This is the book that has probably had the greatest influence on me as an experienced leader, and it has also inspired me to write the book you are reading today. Being able to see possibilities doesn't come naturally—it is an art that we have to cultivate. The book is filled with amazing stories and exercises. I have given it as a gift to my management team, as an invitation and permission to be themselves.

The Alchemist by Paulo Coelho
Coelho's book has been an inspiration to me, my family, and to this book. It has helped me realize the importance of finding my personal mission in life; it has helped me figure out why I am here and what I want to accomplish as a leader.

OTHER BOOKS I RECOMMEND

The Power of Now by Eckhart Tolle

A New Earth: Awakening to Your Life's Purpose by Eckhart Tolle

The Shadow Effect: Illuminating the Hidden Power of Your True Self by
Deepak Chopra, Debbie Ford, and Marianne Williamson

The Mentor's Guide by Lois J. Zachary

The Artist's Way by Julia Cameron

Leadership isn't any longer a matter of finding answers in a book. It comes from the inside and is all about who I am and what I stand for. I still use books as a source of personal inspiration, including spiritual literature and poems about realizing our full potential.

 **Save the Children**